THE OLD TESTAMENT: AN INTRODUCTION

Volume 3
Psalms and Wisdom

Paul Nadim Tarazi

ST VLADIMIR'S SEMINARY PRESS
Crestwood, NY 10707-1699
1996

Library of Congress Cataloging in Publication Data
Tarazi, Paul Nadim, 1943-
  The Old Testament.

  Includes bibliographical references and indexes.
    Contents: v. 1 Historical traditions—v. 2 Prophetic traditions—v. 3 Psalms
and wisdom. 1. Bible. O.T.—Introductions.—I. Title.
BS1140.2.T27   1991   221.6,1   91-26542
ISBN 0-88141-105-1 (v. 1)
ISBN 0-88141-106-X (v. 2)
ISBN 0-88141-107-8 (v. 3)
ISBN 8-00141-108-6 (set)

Volume Table of Contents

ISBN 0-88141-107-8
Set: ISBN 0-88141-108-6

PRINTED IN THE UNITED STATES OF AMERICA

CONTENTS

I—Psalms

II—Wisdom Literature

III—The Old Testament in the Church

Summary Old Testament Chronology

Exodus	Mid-13th century B.C.
Judges	12th and 11th centuries B.C.
Samuel/Saul	End of 11th century B.C.
David/Solomon	10th century until 922 B.C.
Kingdom of Israel	922-722/21 B.C.
Fall of Samaria	715-687 B.C.
Kingdom of Judah	922-587 B.C.
Hezekiah	715-687 B.C.
Manasseh and Amon	687-640 B.C.
Josiah	640-609 B.C.
Deuteronomic Reform	621 B.C.
1st Deportation to Babylon	597 B.C.
Fall of Jerusalem	587 B.C.
End of Babylonian Captivity	538 B.C.
Persian Empire	538-336 B.C.
Macedonian Empire	336-63 B.C.
Macedonian Revolt	164 B.C.

Abbreviations

Books of the Old Testament*

Gen	Genesis	Job	Job	Hab	Habakkuk
Ex	Exodus	Ps	Psalms	Zeph	Zephanaiah
Lev	Leviticus	Prov	Proverbs	Hag	Haggai
Num	Numbers	Eccl	Ecclesiastes	Zech	Zechariah
Deut	Deuteronomy	Song	Song of Solomon	Mal	Malachi
Josh	Joshua	Is	Isaiah	Tob	Tobit
Judg	Judges	Jer	Jeremiah	Jdt	Judith
Ruth	Ruth	Lam	Lamentations	Wis	Wisdom
1 Sam	1 Samuel	Ezek	Ezekiel	Sir	Sirach (Ecclesiasticus)
2 Sam	2 Samuel	Dan	Daniel	Bar	Baruch
1 Kg	1 Kings	Hos	Hosea	1 Esd	1 Esdras
2 Kg	2 Kings	Joel	Joel	2 Esd	1 Esdras
1 Chr	1 Chronicles	Am	Amos	1 Macc	1 Maccabees
2 Chr	2 Chronicles	Ob	Obadiah	2 Macc	2 Maccabees
Ezra	Ezra	Jon	Jonah	3 Macc	3 Maccabees
Neh	Nehemiah	Mic	Micah	4 Macc	4 Maccabees
Esth	Esther	Nah	Nahum		

Books of the New Testament

Mt	Matthew	Eph	Ephesians	Heb	Hebrews
Mk	Mark	Phil	Philippians	Jas	James
Lk	Luke	Col	Colossians	1 Pet	1 Peter
Jn	John	1Thess	1 Thessalonians	2 Pet	2 Peter
Acts	Acts of the Apostles	2 Thess	2 Thessalonians	1 Jn	1 John
Rom	Romans	1 Tim	1 Timothy	2 Jn	2 John
1 Cor	1 Corinthians	2 Tim	2 Timothy	3 Jn	3 John
2 Cor	2 Corinthians	Tit	Titus	Jude	Jude
Gal	Galatians	Philem	Philemon	Rev	Revelation

*Following the larger canon known as the Septuagint.

Foreword

This is the third and last volume of my trilogy of introductions to the Old Testament. It deals with the third collection known as the "Writings." The book is divided into three parts, the first dedicated to the Book of Psalms, the second devoted to Wisdom literature, and the third presenting a conclusion to the entire three-volume series. In the third part I address two controversial yet vitally important issues: the relationship between the two Testaments and the authoritative value of the Old Testament for a Christian.

Like its companion volumes this one presupposes the reader's familiarity with the content of the Old Testament books. It will be helpful that my readers begin by familiarizing themselves with the literature discussed in each part before embarking on reading my comments therein. In any case, it would be advisable that they always consult the biblical passages I refer to in my presentation.

Since my introductions are intended for both general readers and theologians, my constant dilemma is to find the right formula to satisfy both. I hope I have been successful in the previous volumes. In this one, however, the general reader may be over-taxed due to extensive references to Biblical Hebrew. This was necessary since modern translations often use different English words to render the same original Hebrew term, and quite often my argument is based on the original Hebrew. However, reproducing the words as they actually occur in the Hebrew text may not always be helpful to someone unfamiliar with Hebrew because the same word can look quite different in different contexts. Hebrew (as well as all Semitic languages) is consonantal, i.e., its alphabet lacks any symbols for what we call vowels. When we transliterate a Hebrew word, we must make an educated guess as to what those vowels were intended to be, and even if we are correct, there is no consistency in any given word's vowel sounds because they change depending on the word's function in the sentence. In addition, other words such as the definite article, prepositions, and possessive pronouns, to name but a few, are attached to the word they refer to. Where I thought these variations in word structure could be confusing, I resorted to the following device: after transliterating the Hebrew word I added in parentheses either the term in its simplest form including vowels, or sometimes its consonantal root form. These additions are always in bold lettering. It is my hope that by doing this I will allow my readers who do not know Hebrew to recognize the same word in different contexts and thus be able to follow my argument.

Again, my heartfelt thanks to Tom Dykstra who is by now not merely my editor but, to a great extent, my close companion in the production of my works: his professionalism and insistent dedication to making an inherently difficult subject as understandable as possible are remarkable.

Paul Nadim Tarazi

1

Psalms

1

The Origins of Kingship

The book of Psalms frequently portrays God as a heavenly monarch, so in order to understand what is meant by such portrayals one must first understand ancient Hebrew thought about kingship in general. This in turn requires an understanding of how kingship itself came into being. And since the Canaanite kingdoms of Israel and Judah borrowed the conception from their neighbors, it is necessary to consider the matter from the wider perspective of the ancient Near East as a whole.

Tribal Society

The basic nucleus of human existence in the ancient Near East was not the individual, nor even the family, but rather the tribe or clan.[1] A reflection of this can be seen in the Old Testament legal codes for which the ultimate criminal penalty is exclusion from one's people.[2] Such sentences effectively amounted to capital punishment, because life in the wilderness was possible only in oases where water was available—and that is where the tribe lived.[3] As for the tribe itself, its continued existence was possible only so long as order and harmony within it could be maintained,

1. This can be gathered from the fact that the Hebrew term *mišpahah* originally meant clan and later came to mean village as well. The underlying meaning—"the most basic societal unit"—remained unchanged while the actual unit it referred to did change, as the society itself changed from a nomadic (tribe/clan-based) to a sedentary (village-based) existence.
2. See Lev 17:10; 20:3, 5, 6.
3. The consciousness of life's dependence upon water is also reflected in the fact that deities—viewed as masters of human life and thus life-giving—were often worshipped at water sources (springs or streams) or near trees or groves (vegetation is a sure sign of the presence of water). See Deut 12:2; Jer 2:20; 3:6, 13;17:2; Ezek 6:13; 20:28.

and this in turn could be ensured only if its members were strictly bound together by a single *arkhe,* or source of authority. This ultimate authority was the person of the tribal or clan patriarch.[4] Any disobedience, any revolt against his will or rulings dealt a blow against the very root of society and threatened its existence.[5] Conversely, obedience ensured the society's survival. In this sense, it was the patriarch who de facto supported his tribe and not vice versa. In this task he was aided immensely by the memory of the founding patriarch or patriarchs:

1) A tribe is known by the name of its forefather. The names "Israel" and "Jacob" can refer either to the person or the tribe whose forefather he became,[6] while the word "Israelites" in English translations of the Bible refers directly to the forefather since this word renders the Hebrew *bene yisra'el* which literally means "sons/children of Israel."

2) Consequently, the history of a tribe, or at least the history of its origins, is recounted as the forefather's life story. Moreover, this story is not merely a preamble to the history of the tribe itself but is normative for the tribe's self-understanding, an essential part of its identity.[7] Though presented as a history of past events, this is a special kind of history that also expresses the tribe's understanding of its future destiny as well; it is as if the entire fate of the tribe were already settled forever in the life of the patriarch.[8] And for

---

4. The Greek *patriarches* is a combination of *patria* (clan or tribe, based on *pater* which means "father") and *arkhe* (origin, source, rule, authority). Thus, "patriarch" literally means a "father figure" who has absolute (fatherly) authority over all members of a given tribe throughout time as well as space. This connotation of authority can also be found in the word "matriarch" which has the same etymology as "patriarch."

5. See vol. 2, p.33.

6. References to Jacob or Israel as a person are numerous and self-evident; for uses of those names to mean the entire tribe, see, e.g. Ps 78:5, 21, 55-59, 71.

7. In a similar manner, Americans include the adventures of the "pilgrims" between England, the Netherlands, and the shores of Massachusetts as an integral part of their own history (see vol.1, p.14) and even as exemplary of the spirit of religious freedom essential to their own self-understanding.

8. If I may be allowed the use of modern terminology, the patriarch would be, or function as, the DNA of his progeny.

that reason this special kind of story must respond to changing needs and changing situations of the tribe. For it to remain relevant it must occasionally be updated by reading back into it determinative events in the life of the tribe that actually happened long after the patriarch's death. For example, Abraham's life story was made to reflect the events of the exodus that happened centuries after his death, since the exodus became an essential part of Israel's self-understanding. At the outset of Abraham's sojourn in Canaan we are told that: (a) "Now there was a *famine in the land*. So Abram *went down to Egypt* to sojourn there, for the famine was severe in the land" (Gen 12:10); (b) "But the Lord *afflicted Pharaoh* and his house *with great plagues* because of Sarai, Abram's wife" (v.17); and (c) "So Abram *went up from Egypt,* he and his wife, and all that he had, and Lot with him, into the Negeb." (13:1) This is all exodus terminology, as one can see from the references to famine, plagues, and going down to and up from Egypt in Gen 42:3; 43:4-5; 46:3-4; 47:4, 13; Ex 12:37-38; 13:18b.

3) The organic nature of the interrelationship between forefather and tribe can be seen in the fact that a statement addressed to the former applies to the latter (see Gen 49 and Deut 33).

4) The absolute authority of a patriarch for his tribe finds its most compelling expression in the *oneness* of each tribal forefather. Whenever a clan or even a whole tribe joins with another tribe, one of them must relinquish its original forebear and come to be known by the name of the other.[9] Conversely, when a tribe grows and geographically expands to the extent that its oneness, and thus its very life, can no longer be guaranteed by a single authority, it may split into two tribes with a new eponym for each. This split is so real that the two new entities behave as if they were two *originally* independent ones and can even become deadly enemies who view their enmity as extending back to the ancient past. The most striking example in the Bible is the story of the kingdom of

9. See vol.1, pp.17-21.

Edom and its relationship with Judah and Israel. The animosity between the former and the latter, especially Judah,[10] is read back into the lives of their *twin* progenitors, its origins being traced back to when they were still in their mother's womb (Gen 25:21-26; 27-28; 32-33)! Another telling example is the case of Joseph's sons, Manasseh and Ephraim. The split of the Joseph tribe into two necessitated the inclusion among the original Israelite patriarchs (i.e., Jacob's sons) of these two—and only these two—grandsons (Gen 48); even the subsequent ascendancy of Ephraim over Manasseh was accounted for in this retrospective reading of history (vv.13-20). The inclusion of the two grandsons de facto eliminated Joseph, Jacob's son, from the list of Jacob's progeny on the tribal level. In other words, Manasseh and Ephraim became the "brothers" of their uncle Benjamin. The Manassehites and the Ephraimites were thus as much *bene yisra'el* (children of Israel/Jacob) as the Benjaminites were.

The Tribal Deity

The tribal patriarch played a similarly important role in the tribe's religion, with the forefather functioning as the original link between the tribe members and the deity they revered, and each patriarch serving to renew and perpetuate that link. It is not difficult to understand how this relationship developed. The essential characteristic of any human concept of godhead is that the deity bestows and ensures life. And since life can undergo no interruption without ceasing to be life, the deity must have granted it to the tribe beginning with the forefather, prototype of all subsequent patriarchs. Hence, all traditional stories of the early days of tribes start with an encounter between the forefather and the deity, whereby the latter appears to the former in an "epiphany" or "theophany," and the former acknowledges and bears witness to this event by building a shrine that becomes throughout the generations the place of meeting between the tribe and its

10. See vol.2, pp. 30-31, 192-193, 200.

deity. A typical instance is the case of Abra(ha)m and the altar at Bethel that was the central shrine of the kingdom of Israel:[11]

> Then the Lord appeared to Abram and said, "To your descendants I will give this land." So he built there an altar to the Lord, who had appeared to him. Thence he removed to the mountain on the east of Bethel and pitched his tent, with Bethel on the west and Ai on the east; and there he built an altar to the Lord and called upon his name. (Gen 12:7-8)

> And he [Abram] journeyed on from the Negeb as far as Bethel, to the place where his tent had been at the beginning, between Bethel and Ai, to the place where he had made an altar at the first; and there Abram called on the name of the Lord. (13:3-4)

This double linkage between the deity and the forefather on the one hand, and *simultaneously* between the deity and its place of original epiphany[12] on the other hand, can be seen in the story of Jacob and Bethel:

> Jacob...came to a certain place and stayed there that night, because the sun had set. Taking one of the stones of the place, he put it under his head and lay down in that place to sleep. And he dreamed...and behold, the Lord...said, "I am the Lord, *the God of Abraham your father* and the God of Isaac; the land on which you lie I will give to you and your descendants; and your descendants shall be like the dust of the earth[13]... and by you and your descendants shall all the families of the earth bless themselves/be blessed.[14] Behold, I am with you and will keep you wherever you go, and will bring you back to this land; for I will not leave you until I have done that which I have spoken to you." Then Jacob awoke from his sleep and said, "*Surely the Lord is in this place; and I did not know it.*" And he was afraid, and said, "How awesome is this place! This is none other than *the house of God,*[15] and this is the gate of heaven." So Jacob rose early in the morning, and he took the stone which he had put under his head and set it up for a pillar and

11. See vol.1 p.71.
12. A striking example of the latter is the case of Elijah who, when confronted with the major crisis of his life, was directed to journey all the way to Mount Horeb in order to meet the Lord and hear him speak (1 Kg 19)!
13. See Gen 13:16a.
14. See Gen 13:12:3b.
15. That is, the temple/shrine of God, which is the gate to heaven where God is seated on his heavenly throne.

poured oil on top of it. He called the name of that place Bethel;[16] but the name of the city was Luz at first. Then Jacob made a vow, saying, "If God will be with me, and will keep me in this way that I go, and will give me bread to eat and clothing to wear, so that I come again to my father's house in peace, then *the Lord shall be my God*, and this stone, which I have set as a pillar, shall be *God's house*." (Gen 28:10-22)

God said to Jacob, "Arise, go up to Bethel, and dwell there; and *make there an altar to the God who appeared to you* when you fled from your brother Esau." So Jacob said to his household and to all who were with him, "Put away the foreign gods that are among you,[17]...then let us arise and go up to Bethel, that I may make an altar to *the God who answered me in the day of my distress* and has been with me wherever I have gone."[18]...And Jacob came to Luz (that is, Bethel)...and there he built an altar, and called the place El-bethel,[19] *because there God had revealed himself to him* when he fled from his brother...God *appeared to Jacob again,* when he came from Padan-Aram,[20] and blessed him. And God said to him, "...no longer shall your name be Jacob, but Israel shall be your name...I am God Almighty; be fruitful and multiply; a nation and a company of nations shall come from you, and kings shall spring from you. The land which I gave to *Abraham* and Isaac I will give you, and I will give the land to *your descendants* after you."[21] Then God went up from him in the place where he had spoken with him. And Jacob set up a pillar in the place where he had spoken with him, a pillar of stone; and he poured out a drink offering on it, and poured oil on it. So Jacob called the name of the place where God had spoken with him, Bethel. (35:1-15)

The story identifies the God of Jacob as not only the God of Bethel, but the God of Abraham as well. Thus, reference is made to an earlier divine epiphany in order to establish the identity of the deity being referred to at a later time. The original epiphany of a deity is by the same token its primary "defining" manifestation;

16. The Hebrew *bet'el* means "the house of El/God," which is how Jacob refers to it in v.17, the Hebrew there being *bet 'elohim*.

17. Compare with Josh 24:2, 14-16; i.e., this is another example of an exodus event being read back into the life of a patriarch.

18. See Gen 28:20-22.

19. That is, (the) God of Bethel.

20. Where he sojourned with his uncle Laban (Gen 28:1-7).

21. See Gen 17:1-8; 28:3-4.

in it the deity introduces itself by referring *exclusively* to what it will do in the future. In contrast, subsequent epiphanies usually refer back to the original one in order to ensure that the person to whom the deity is manifesting itself is aware of the deity's identity. God first manifested himself to Abraham, and that is why at that time he only made promises for the future—and from that time forward he would always be identified first and foremost as the God of Abraham.[22] In other words, Abraham is an integral part of the "definition" of the God of Jacob/Israel and his descendants. And each of those descendants knows this God as "the God of *my father*" just as Jacob/Israel himself did,[23] since the tribal patriarch was understood to be the father of the entire tribe.

But in a culture that was not yet monotheistic, what was to prevent Israel from worshiping multiple Gods—a God of Jacob and a God of Abraham who were believed to be two separate deities? This would not be unthinkable, and neither Abraham nor Jacob could personally guarantee the oneness of the deity. Only the Lord himself could do that—and it is he who does it. It is he who promises to be the God of Abraham's descendants (Gen 17:8), and it is he who makes himself *also* the God of Jacob (28:21; 35:2-4). In other words, the real link between Jacob and Abraham lies in the *same* blessing of the same God, as is crystal clear from a comparison of Gen 17:1-8; 28:3-4; and 35:9-15. It is this God who makes a patriarch out of each of Abraham, Isaac, and Jacob, through his promises to multiply their descendants. Actually, as the book of Genesis relates, it is not Abraham who begets Isaac to make it possible for God to realize His promise of blessing, rather it is God who grants to Abraham Isaac so that he—Abraham—may share in the blessing![24]

22. "The God of Abraham, Isaac, and Jacob" in Ex 3:6, 15, 16; 4:5; 6:3. "The God of Abraham and Isaac" in Gen 28:13; 32:9; 48:15; also 31:42. Just "the God of Abraham." in Gen 26:24.

23. See Gen 31:42; 32:9; also Gen 26:24; 28:13; Ex 3:6, 15. The same applies to a servant who would refer to his deity as the "God of my master" (Gen 24:12, 27, 42, 48).

24. Gen 15:1-6; 17:15-22; 18:9-15; 21:1-7.

On the other hand, however, while this God is able to "voyage through time" from patriarch to patriarch and to their descendants, he does not seem to have the same capability when it comes to space. He seems rather to be "organically" linked with a given place,[25] which in the passage quoted above is Bethel. It is as though he had to appear to Jacob specifically at Bethel in order to make sure that Jacob would accept him as the God of *Abraham!* And this is only natural since He *is* the God *of Bethel* (Gen 28:16-17, 19:35:7, 15). This is so important that in order to ensure that Jacob would not confound Him with any of the other deities around,[26] He had to introduce himself in Padan-Aram as "the God of Bethel, *where you anointed a pillar and made a vow to me."* (Gen 31:13a)[27]

But aside from the tribal god's association with a particular place and particular patriarchs, what was he like? In other words, in what other ways would a tribe member describe his god? The answer is that in the ancient Near East people thought of their God primarily in anthropomorphic terms, just as we tend to do ourselves. Since we can only describe things using human terminology, it is only natural that this terminology has an effect on the way we think about things as well. The effect can even be seen when we are speaking about tangible realities, such as minerals, vegetation, or animals—in these cases we tend to underline the differences, and thus what they are not, compared to us.[28] The reason is that tangible realities can be described fairly directly in terms immediately related to sense perceptions; their differences from us are immediately apparent. With intangibles, the opposite happens: we tend to speak of them more anthropomorphically, i.e., in human terms. The reason lies in our need first to define

25. See vol.1, pp.39-40, 43-44.
26. See Gen 35:2, 4.
27. See Gen 28:18-22.
28. For instance, we say that a dog cannot speak, a tree cannot move, a stone does not feel, and in each case it is understood that we mean "as we humans do."

them positively, i.e., make them "real"—quasi-tangible—for us, before we can even begin to describe the differences between them and us. To name a few examples of the way we anthropomorphize common actions, often without even realizing it ourselves, consider statements such as: "I was touched by her thoughtfulness." "I could see the catastrophe coming." "I see what you mean." "I could smell the danger." "I changed my mind." "I overstepped my rights and overlooked his." "I turned the odds around." "The thought crossed my mind." "I reached out to them." "You light up my life." The intangible is described in terms of the tangible, and this process is as inevitable for us today as it was for our ancestors thousands of years ago.

The same principle applies to descriptions of the deity. We choose the closest possible tangible reality that reflects the essential qualities or features we ascribe to the deity. In other words, we name it according to the closest tangible reality that expresses the relation we perceive to exist between the deity and ourselves. In tribal societies, that closest relationship would be the one between the member of the tribe and its patriarch, whether forefather or actual tribe leader. The reason is simple and lies in what I said earlier concerning life being the basic characteristic of the notion of godhead. Life, in the tribal experience, is essentially linked to the person of the patriarch: it originates with the forefather and continues due to the realm of harmony and order guaranteed by the tribe leader who is thus perceived as its "father." In other words, the abstract notion of life itself is, in the mind of the tribe member, channeled through the tangible reality of the person of the patriarch perceived as "father." Having life is equivalent to being "fathered," i.e., having been brought into life from the realm of non-existence as well as nurtured daily so as not to succumb to the ever-threatening realm of death and non-existence. It is no wonder then that the abstract notion "life" was linked to the concrete designation *'ab* (father), which is taken from the terminology of the smallest—and thus most immediately tangible—societal unit one experiences, the family. Indeed, the patriarch was known as *'ab*, and so was the deity.[29]

Kingship

More permanent settlements than the oases were erected on the seashores or along the river banks where water, the most necessary element for the maintenance of life, was in abundance and could support a larger number of people.[30] When compared to a gathering of movable dwellings such as tents, establishing and maintaining a city entails the much more complex task of erecting buildings and surrounding walls. This more complex and "artificial" nature of a city necessitated a new form of human bonds and order, which in turn required a new form of government. Whereas in tribal society any person did, or at least could and had the time to, perform all activities required to sustain life,[31] the more complex expression of life in a city required a certain level of specialization and, by the same token, the emergence of "professionals," such as merchants, carpenters, masons, teachers, cult servers, administrators, and the like. This new situation transformed society, creating new relationships between people that transcended the old ties of family, clan, and tribe.[32] It is understandable how such an "artificial" society would require a "nonnatural"[33] leader who would either be elected or take the reins of

---

29. See e.g. Gen 17:4, 5; Ps 68:5; 89:26; 103:13.
30. Notice the location of the large cities throughout history, such as Memphis, Babylon, Antioch, Alexandria, Ephesus, Rome, Paris, London, Stockholm, Copenhagen, Moscow, Vienna, Budapest, Belgrade, Boston, New York, Chicago, Philadelphia, Pittsburgh, St Louis, Toronto, Montreal, Vancouver.
31. Such as shepherding, fruit picking, gardening, cooking, and defending oneself in battle.
32. The new clans became the guilds. It is true that the tendency was, as usual in life, to follow the less complex path; thus, the children of merchants would be merchants, and so on. However, the door was open for the phenomenon of "adoption" to take place on the basis of joining a profession rather than a clan or tribe; and the more complex a society becomes, the more the social divisions tend to be along the line of professions; hence the new societal units of guilds and professional "associations."
33. By this I mean someone who is not a "given" by the basic nature of human relations, i.e., clan or tribe.

government by force and then be recognized by the populace. This new leader came to be called "king."

Still, the new societal unit of the city could only be understood along the same lines as the essential human societal unit, the clan or tribe. Consequently, the king was understood as the patriarch or *'ab* (father) of the nation, and his role was not merely to rule but to maintain order and harmony among his people, just as a patriarch would do for his tribe:

> May he [the king] judge thy people with righteousness,
>   and thy poor with justice! ...
> May he defend the cause of the poor of the people,
> give deliverance to the needy,
> and crush the oppressor! ...
> For he delivers the needy when he calls,
> the poor and him who has no helper.
> He has pity on the weak and the needy,
> and saves the lives of the needy.
> From oppression and violence he redeems their life;
> and precious is their blood in his sight. (Ps 72:2, 4, 12-14)

> He [the expected king] shall not judge by what his eyes see,
>   or decide by what his ears hear;
> but with righteousness he shall judge the poor,
> and decide with equity for the meek of the earth;
> and he shall smite the earth with the rod of his mouth,
> and with the breath of his lips he shall slay the wicked. (Is 11:3b-5)[34]

Not only would the king show fatherly concern for the welfare of his people, but also, through the very fact of his existence as king, he functioned as the source and sustainer of all life in his kingdom. A kingdom without a king could not survive, just as a tribe without a patriarch would disintegrate. Therefore, the welfare of the king was identical with the welfare of his people:

> Let the mountains bear prosperity for the people,
>   and the hills, in righteousness!

34. See also 2 Sam 12:1-6; 1 Kg 3:16-28.

> May he [the king] live while the sun endures,
> and as long as the moon, throughout all generations!
> May he be like rain that falls on the mown grass,
> like showers that water the earth!
> In his days may righteousness flourish,
> and peace abound, till the moon be no more!
> May there be abundance of grain in the land;
> on the tops of the mountains may it wave;
> may its fruit be like Lebanon;
> and may men blossom forth from the cities
> like the grass of the field! (Ps 72:3, 5-7, 16)

That is why, in Ps 144, his prayer for *personal* victory over his enemies concludes with a petition for fullness of blessings over people and land alike:

> [O God] who givest victory to *kings*:
> who rescuest *David* thy servant.
> Rescue *me* from the cruel sword,
> and deliver *me* from the hand of aliens,
> whose mouths speak lies,
> and whose right hand is a right hand of falsehood.
> May *our* sons in their youth
> be like plants full grown,
> *our* daughters like corner pillars
> cut for the structure of a palace;
> may *our* garners be full,
> providing all manner of store;
> may *our* sheep bring forth thousands
> and ten thousands in our fields;
> may *our* cattle be heavy with young,
> suffering no mischance or failure in bearing;
> may there be no cry of distress in *our* streets!
> Happy the *people* to whom such blessings fall!
> Happy are the *people* whose God is the Lord! (vv. 12-15)

And because the very basis of a city's life depends on the person of the king, unceasing prayer for his long life and good health was essential:

> Long may he live,
> may gold of Sheba be given to him!

> May prayer be made for him continually,
> and blessings invoked for him all the day!
> May his name endure for ever,
> his fame continue as long as the sun!
> May men bless themselves by him,
> all nations call him blessed! (Ps 72:15, 17)

But since actual experience showed that the king was, after all, as mortal as everyone else, the permanence of the kingly presence was secured through dynasty, which is therefore an essential component of the notion of kingship. This is why when God makes a permanent covenant with David it applies to the king's dynasty as much as to the king personally, and promises spoken to the king personally are effectively spoken to each of his successors:

> The Lord swore to David a sure oath
> from which he will not turn back:
> "One of the sons of your body
> I will set on your throne.
> If your sons keep my covenant
> and my testimonies which I shall teach them,
> their sons also for ever
> shall sit upon your throne." (Ps 132:11-12)[35]

> He [David] shall cry to me, "Thou art my Father,
> my God, and the Rock of my Salvation."
> And I will make him the first-born,
> the highest of the kings of the earth.
> My steadfast love I will keep for him for ever,
> and my covenant will stand firm for him.
> I will establish his line for ever
> and his throne as the days of the heavens.
> If his children forsake my law
> and do not walk according to my ordinances,
> if they violate my statutes
> and do not keep my commandments,
> then I will punish their transgression with the rod
> and their iniquity with scourges;
> but I will not remove from him my steadfast love,

35. See also Ps 45:16; 2 Sam 7:1-17//1 Chr 17:1-15.

or be false to my faithfulness.
I will not violate my covenant,
or alter the word that went forth from my lips.
Once for all I have sworn by my holiness;
I will not lie to David.
His line shall endure for ever,
his throne as long as the sun before me.
Like the moon it shall be established for ever;
it shall stand firm while the skies endure. (Ps 89:26-37)

Such texts reflect a belief that the permanence of the king(ship) was what ensured the permanence of the people, and not vice versa.

The Deity As King

As was the case in tribal society, the notion of deity in ancient Near Eastern civilization[36] was conceived along the lines of the person of the ruler, the king in this instance. Even a cursory reading of the Old Testament, especially the book of Psalms, will convince the reader of this fact, since it is full of proclamations such as: "The Lord is king for ever and ever" (Ps 10:16a); "Who is the King of glory? The Lord, strong and mighty, the Lord, mighty in battle! Who is this King of glory? The Lord of hosts, he is the King of glory!" (24:8, 10); "The Lord sits enthroned as king for ever" (29:10b); "Thou art my King and my God" (44:4a; also 68:24; 74:12; 84:3; 145:1); "For God is the king of all the earth...God reigns over the nations; God sits on his holy throne" (47:7-8); "For the Lord is a great God, and a great King above all gods" (95:3); "...make a joyful noise before the King, the Lord!" (98:6b).[37]

Clearly, we must understand what people thought of their king in order to understand what they thought of their God. Thus, one way to help us understand the biblical God would be to begin by studying the characteristics ascribed to kings in bibli-

36. The term civilization itself originates from the Latin *civitas* (nation; city).
37. See also Is 6:5; 41:21; 43:15; 44:6; Jer 8:19; 10:6-7, 10; 48:15; 51;57; Mic 2:13; Zeph 3:15; Zech 14:9, 16, 17.

cal and ancient Near Eastern extra-biblical materials and then show how those characteristics applied to God. We could also proceed more directly by studying the psalms that refer to him as king, thereby simultaneously learning about the biblical understandings of kingship and deity. I shall adopt the second approach since it is simpler and better fits the introductory nature and space limitations of this volume; however, so that this will be an essentially complete and well-rounded presentation of the biblical conceptions of God and king, I shall also on occasion appeal to other biblical passages or extra-biblical sources on subjects not adequately covered by the psalms.

2

Kingly Victory

A good point of departure for our investigation is Psalm 93.[1] This text presents a general description of God as king, unencumbered by any specific reference to his dealings with the human realm, be it Israel or Judah, Israelite or Judahite kings, the wicked within his people, or even the foreign nations or their deities. In other words, this psalm will allow us to have an idea of the most basic constituent of the notion of divine kingship and, by inference, of human kingship.

V.1 The Lord reigns, he is robed in majesty;
The Lord is robed, he is girded with strength.
The world is surely established; it shall never be shaken;

The Hebrew verb *malak* (reigned/reigns) in this verse presents the translator with some difficulties. The Hebrew past perfect refers to an action completed in the past but with effects carrying into the future, so that depending on context it may be translated into either past or present tense in English. "Reigned" or "has reigned" are possibilities but suggest the Lord's reign at some time came to an end, which certainly does not fit the context. "The Lord is king" would solve that problem but sounds like a mere affirmation of Yahweh's royal status, a thought that would have been expressed by the Hebrew *yahweh melek*, i.e., literally "the Lord is king."[2] "The Lord has become king"

1. A more detailed version of this chapter was originally published as the article "An Exegesis of Psalm 93" in *St. Vladimir's Theological Quarterly* 35 (1991) 137-148.

2. Chances are very slim that *mlk* represents the nominal rather than the verbal form of the word. The Masoretic tradition has consistently vocalized it as a verb, that reading

17

is somewhat better because it reflects the Hebrew verb's notion of a specific past action through which the Lord established himself as king, but it too merely affirms Yahweh's royal status without adequately conveying the verb's emphasis on reigning as an ongoing action.

The verb's intended meaning in this context may be clarified by investigating its use in other, similar contexts. Since appealing directly to other occurrences of *yahweh malak* in the Psalms might easily become a circular argument, it is advisable to start with material extraneous to this book. Two texts provide almost perfect parallels:

> But Absalom sent secret messengers throughout all the tribes of Israel, saying, As soon as you hear the sound of the trumpet, then shout: Absalom reigns (*malak absalom*) at Hebron! (2 Sam 15:10)

> So he [Jehu] said, This is just what he [the prophet sent by Elisha] said to me: 'Thus says the Lord, I anoint you king over Israel.' Then hurriedly they all took their cloaks and spread them for him on the bare steps; and they blew the trumpet and proclaimed, Jehu reigns (*malak yehu*). (2 Kings 9:12f)

These two call to mind a third:

> There Zadok the priest took the horn of oil from the tent and anointed Solomon. Then they blew the trumpet, and all the people said, Long live King Solomon! And all the people went up following him, playing on pipes and rejoicing with great joy, so that the earth quaked at their noise...When Joab heard the sound of the trumpet,...Jonathan answered Adonijah,...Solomon now sits on the royal throne. And the king [David] went on to pray thus, 'Blessed be the Lord, the God of Israel, who today has granted one of my offspring to sit on my throne ...'
> (1 Kings 1:39f, 41, 43, 46, 48)

The same three elements of trumpet sound, joy, and sitting on the throne that accompany the acclamation of Solomon as king are also found in psalms proclaiming God's kingship.[3] Of the three, the first two are peripheral, while the third is actually the direct

---

is confirmed by the Septuagint and other pre-Masoretic Greek translations, and the three following colons are parallel to the first and all use perfect verbs.

3. Ps 47:5; 98:6 for the trumpet sound; Ps 68:3; 96:11; 97:1, 8 for joy; and Ps 47:8; 99:1 for the sitting on the throne.

expression of kingship itself. Indeed, in the text relating to Solomon, nowhere do we read that he *malak* (reigned/reigns), only that he *yašab* (sat/sits) on the throne and that David thanks God for granting him to see his son *yošeb* (sitting) on his throne. This indicates that "sitting on the throne" is a synonym of "reigning," a relationship explicitly confirmed by two psalms: "God reigns over the nations; God sits on his holy throne" (47:8); "The Lord reigns, let the peoples tremble! He sits upon the cherubim; let the earth quake!" (99:1)

Obviously, the idea of sitting on the throne does not refer merely to a past action, in the sense of he once sat down on the throne, but rather that the king has ascended the throne and is still sitting there. The stress is on the completeness of the action and the permanence of its results rather than the temporal connotation that it was a past action. The ancient translations seem to agree with this interpretation in that they all render *yašab* with the present tense "sits." Since, then, the *malak* is to be taken in the same sense as the *yašab*, the best possible translation of *yahweh malak* is: The Lord reigns.[4] Moreover, since the following three perfect verbs refer to the same event, it follows that they should also be translated in the present tense in English.

The word *ge'ut* translated "majesty" in the immediately following phrase has the connotation of something high or lifted up, and thus of grandeur or pride. This can be gathered from its use in completely different contexts. In Ps 17:10 one's enemies are those who "close their hearts to pity; with their mouths they speak *bege'ut* (with arrogance)." In Is 28:1-3 we read about the *'ateret*

---

4. The need to render the psalm as poetry restricts our freedom in translating here. Otherwise, one could more accurately say, "the Lord reigns *indeed*," which is the better translation of *malak* in 2 Sam 15:10 and 2 Kings 9:13. On the other hand, the rule in Semitic languages is that the verb precedes the subject, and emphasis is intended whenever the noun comes first. Thus, our text may also mean: "It is *the Lord* who reigns." This may well be the psalmist's intention, since this psalm was recited at an occasion where the Lord was proclaimed in the Jerusalem temple as the only God of the people.

ge'ut (crown of pride). Is 9:18 refers to the *ge'ut* (height) of smoke, while Is 12:5 speaks of God's deeds as *ge'ut*. Most interesting is the psalm recorded in Isaiah 26: after saying that the wicked deal perversely because they do not *see* the *ge'ut* (majesty) of the Lord (v. 10), the author says they do not *see* His lifted hand that is going to hurl consuming fire over them and bring peace and blessings to His people. (vv.11-15) Thus, *ge'ut* reflects the actual power to rule and is not just external apparel; it is, as it were, implemented majesty.

This conclusion is confirmed by the fact that *labeš* (he robed himself/is robed) is in the same perfect tense as *malak*; the two parts of the first colon thus mean essentially the same thing. Moreover, the second colon takes up the same verb labeš and uses it in parallel with *'oz yit'azzar* (he girded himself with strength/ victory), so a study of this last expression will shed more light on both parallel phrases from the first colon. The verb *hit'azzar* (he girded himself) is clearly a military term as can be seen in Is 8:9: "Band together, you people, and be dismayed; listen, all you far countries; gird yourselves (*hit'azzeru*) and be dismayed." [5] The noun *'oz* also bears the connotation of a (military) victory over adversaries. See Psalms 21 and 86 where *'oz* occurs in parallel with *yešu'ah* (victory, or salvation based on victory) in a military set-ting.[6] One should also add in this connection that the verb *labeš* (to robe oneself), which occurs here with *ge'ut* (majesty), is used twice in Isaiah 59:17 to signify the putting on of military apparel in preparation for victory: "He put on (*wayyilbaš*)[7] righteousness as a breastplate, and a helmet of victory/salvation (*yešu'ah*) on his head; he put on (*wayyilbaš*) garments of vengeance for clothing, and wrapped himself in fury as in a mantle."

All of the above clearly shows that the series *malak, ge'ut labeš,*

---

5. The military connotation can also be seen in another form of the verb (*'azar*, he girded) in Ps 18:39: "For you girded me (*watte'azzereni*) with strength for the battle; you made my assailants sink under me."

6. Ps 21:1, 8-12 and 86:9, 14, 16. See also 1 Sam 2:1-10; Ps 68:1f; 21, 28, 30; Ps 89:19.

7. From *labeš*.

labeš, and *'oz hit'azzar*, refers to the Lord's establishing himself as king through victory over his enemy. The psalmist is not speaking abstractly of the notion of kingship but is acknowledging that the Lord is in reality enacting his rule and dominion over a real enemy that he has reduced to powerlessness. His victory is total and final; its outcome is the establishment of the world in such a way that it shall never be shaken. A survey of the use of *tebel* (world) in the Old Testament indicates it specifically refers to the world of human beings:

1) Twenty-four out of 36[8] times *tebel* clearly refers to the human beings dwelling in the world, i.e., to the world as the inhabited world.

2) A case can also be made for the same meaning in 1 Sam 2:8c and Chr 16:30b. The first is part of Hannah's song (vv. 1-10) that speaks of God's dealings with men (especially v. 8f). The second is word for word identical to Ps 93:1c and appears in a context (vv. 28-31) where men are asked to ascribe glory to the Lord (v. 29c).

3) In the ten remaining occurrences[9] *tebel* can be taken to mean the inhabited world.

The context of *tebel* here in Ps 93:1c is most like the context of 1 Chr 16:30b and Ps 96:10b since in both of the latter we also find *yahweh malak* (1 Chr 16:31b and Ps 96:10a). In the second of these *tebel* unequivocally means "inhabited world," and in the first that meaning seems likely, so the case for understanding *tebel* in the same way in Ps 93 is strong. That case can be made even stronger by noting how the verb *nakon/yikkon* (is established) in the Old Testament usually refers to human beings. The thing "established" is God's hand through David, David himself, David's throne, the king's throne, David's house, David's king-

8. Job 18:18; 34:13; Ps 9:8; 19:4; 24:1; 33:8; 50:12; 89:11; 96:10, 13; 98:7, 9; Is 13:11; 14:17, 21; 18:3; 26:9, 18; 27:6; 34:1; Lam 4:12; Nah 1:5; and Prov 8:31 to which one can safely add v. 26 since it pertains to the same context.

9. 2 Sam 22:16; Job 37:12; Ps 18:15; 77:18; 90:2; 93:1; 97:4; Is 24:4; Jer 10:12//15:15.

dom, man, man's seed, man's ways, man's lips, man's thoughts, man's purpose, the slanderer, the congregation of Jacob, or the inhabited mountain of the Lord's temple.[10] Just once (in Ps 93) it refers to God as king. In other words, it always refers to the human realm, and specifically from the perspective of its being "put in order" under God, either directly or indirectly. In the latter case, this order is secured through the mediacy of either the king as the Lord's representative, or wisdom that has its ultimate source in Him.

The steadfastness of this establishment of the world is underscored through the negative assertion *bal-timmot* (it shall not be shaken). The imperfect[11] *yimmot* (is shaken) almost always occurs with the negative *bal or lo',*[12] so the connotation is a positive one: unshakable, secure. Most of the time we find with it an expression indicating the situation is to stand for good.[13] Prov 12:3 shows how close in meaning are *yikkon* and *bal-timmot*: "A man is not established by wickedness, but the root of the righteous will never be moved."[14]

---

10. 1 Sam 7:16; 20:31; 2 Sam 7:26; 1 Kings 2:12, 45f; 1 Chr 17:14, 24; Job 21:8; Ps 89:21, 37; Ps 102:28; 140:11; Prov 4:26; 12:19: 16:3, 12; 20:18; 25:5; 29:14; Is 2:2//Mic 4:1; Jer 30:20.
11. The Hebrew imperfect corresponds to our "continuous" in describing an ongoing action, whether in the present, future, or past.
12. 1 Chr 16:30//Ps 93:1//Ps 96:10//Ps 104:5; Job 41:23; Ps 10:6; 15:5; 21:7; 30:6; 46:5; 62:2, 6; 112:6; 125:1; Prov 10:30; 12:3; Is 40:20; 41:7. The only instances where this verb occurs in the affirmative are Ps 13:4 and 82:5.
13. *ledor wador* (Ps 10:6); *le'olam* (Ps 15:5; 30:6; 112:6; 125:1; Prov 10:30); *tamid* (Ps 16:8); *'olam wa'ed* (Ps 21:6; 104:5); *la'ad* (Ps 21:8).
14. The close correspondence between *yikkon* and the negated *yimmot* can also be seen in the fact that the latter too is usually used with reference to the human realm: the king, the righteous, God's city, the world, and the earth. See 1 Chr 16:30//Ps 93:1//Ps 96:10; Ps 10:6; 15:5; 16:8; 21:7; 30:6; 46:5; 104:5; 112:6; 125:1; Prov 10:30; 12:3.

V.2 *Your throne was established from of old;*
from everlasting you are.

This is not a mere repetition of v.1; rather, it is a declaration of the psalmist's faith that Yahweh did not assume kingship in a near past when He, as it were, restructured the foundations of a world that was on the verge of collapsing. To the contrary, the Lord's throne was *me'az* (from of old), i.e., from the beginning. In other words, the reference here is to the first and only establishment of the world. This can also be seen in the use of *me'az* (from of old) and *me'olam* (from everlasting) here. Moreover, normal Hebrew syntax calls for the pronoun to come first and the predicate second ("you are from everlasting"), but here the order is inverted ("from everlasting you are"), clearly for the purpose of emphasizing the Lord himself. The same emphasis is manifest in the structure of the unit comprised of vv.1-2: having begun with the emphatic *yahweh*,[15] the psalmist ends with the equally emphatic *'attah* (you), through now with the double *me'az/me'olam* in order to assert God's primacy over everything else.

The idea that the establishment of the world is parallel—and thus equivalent—to the establishment of the divine throne (Ps 93:1b-2a) is common to the ancient Near East and is also reflected in Ugaritic literature of that time about the god Baal. A god by definition had to have a kingly residence; in the following story Baal begs his sister Anat to plead with their father El that a temple be built for Baal:[16]

> So, young men, go in!
>   Bow yourselves down before Anat,
>   and fall down, abasing yourselves, in her honour!
>   And say to the virgin Anat,
>   present this message to the Yabamat Limim:[17]

15. See n.4.
16. From the translation of Ugaritic myths of Baal by Karl-Heinz Bernhardt, published in Walter Beyerlin, ed., *Near Eastern Religious Texts Relating to the Old Testament*, (OTL), Philadelphia, 1978, pp.192-221.
17. A name for the goddess Anat

'Message of the mighty Baal,
a word from the one who is exalted among the heroes! ...
I wish to build a palace the like of which the heavens do not know, ...
Come quickly, for I truly will establish it
In the midst of my mountain, (I) the god of Zaphon,
in the holy precinct, on the hill which I possess,
in a pleasant place, on the hill which displays my power.'[18]

The [virgin] Anat retorted:
'The Bull El, [my father], will agree,
he will agree with me and...'[19]

Then Bull El, her father, truly cried out aloud,
El, the king, who created her;
Ashirat[20] and her sons cried out,
the goddess and the horde of her kin:
'Alas, Baal does not have a house like the gods,
an abode like the sons of Ashirat,
a dwelling-place (like) El,
an abode (like) [his sons],...'[21]

The deity creates or establishes its world or realm. But for it to be
established as a deity it needs to have its own mountain, its own throne
to rule from. This is what the story of Baal is all about, and it illustrates
the common conception that the establishment of the world is inseparable from the establishment of the deity's throne, whether it be Baal in
this Ugaritic text or Yahweh in the Old Testament.

V.3 The currents raised, O Lord,
   the currents raised their roar,
   the currents raised their waves.[22]

V.1 proclaimed God's rule as an actual victory over an enemy, a
victory whose outcome is the firm establishment of the inhabited
world. Now we hear explicitly about the enemy opposed to God,

18. Pp.196-197.
19. Pp.199-200.
20. El's consort.
21. P.201.
22. For this translation see my article.

whose goal is to shatter the world as an ordered realm under Him. An overview of similar Old Testament texts will reveal that this enemy is the primeval Sea, also known under its mythological figure of Leviathan/Rahab/dragon.

Two other texts which identify this enemy are particularly relevant in that they too come from psalms speaking of God's establishment of the world:

> Yet God is my king from of old, working salvation (*yešu'ot*) in the earth. You divided the sea by your might ('*oz*); you broke the heads of the dragons in the waters. You crushed the heads of Leviathan...you established (*hekinota, kun*)[23] the luminaries and the sun. (Ps 74:12-14, 16b)

> You rule the raging (*ge'ut*) of the sea; when its waves rise (*so', nasa'*), you still them. You crushed Rahab like a carcass; you scattered your enemies with your mighty arm (*bizroa' 'uzzeka, 'oz*)...the world and all that is in it—you have founded them. You have a mighty arm; strong (*ta'oz, 'oz*) is your hand, high (*tarum*) is your right hand. (Ps 89:9-10, 11b, 13)

The synonymous parallelism—a basic feature of Hebrew poetry—clearly shows that: (a) Leviathan/Rahab corresponds to the raging sea; (b) the sea raging with its waves acts as God's enemy in threatening the world established by him; and (c) it has an army of "dragons." God's intervention is the containment of Rahab within boundaries[24] so that it would not threaten anew the inhabited world—God's orderly realm—with destruction. The conclusion to be drawn from the close correspondence between the terminology of the above texts and Ps 93 is that the latter is undoubtedly speaking of God's victory over the primeval Sea.

The ferocity of the battle between God and Rahab for supremacy over the world is reflected in the use of the term '*ap* (anger) to describe God's overpowering attack against his enemy and its minions: "God will not turn back his anger; the helpers of Rahab

23. The same verb that appears in Ps 93:2.
24. Job 7:12; 38:4-11; Ps 104:5-9; Prov 8:28f. See also Gen. 1:9.

bowed beneath him." (Job 9-13) This passage immediately brings
to mind another that describes this primeval battle: "Was your
wrath against the rivers, O Lord? Or your anger against the rivers,
or your rage against the sea, when you drove your horses, your
chariots to victory?" (Hab 3:8; see entire poem in vv.2-15) The
parallelism between sea and rivers is encountered elsewhere in Old
Testament poetry within the same context of God's battle against
his enemy.[25] Consequently, Rahab's helpers and Leviathan's "dragons" are none other than the sea rivers or underwater currents.
This conclusion is confirmed by an interesting Ugaritic text[26]
where the god *Yamm* (sea) appears under the parallel name *Nahar*
(river) in the repeated parallelism: *zbl ym tpt nhr* (O Prince Sea, O
Judge River). Also in support of my conclusion is the fact that the
qol (voice/roar) of these rivers is presented in v. 4 as the roar of the
waters (v. 4a), that is, of the sea (v. 4b).

This explains the "roar" of the "currents" here in Ps 93:3, and
that in turn leads to an explanation of *dokyam* (translated "their
waves" above) at the end of the verse. From Jer 51 we learn that
the *qol* (voice/roar) of the sea is the sound of its waves: "The sea
has risen over Babylon; she has been covered by its tumultuous
(*hamon*) waves...Their waves roar (*hamu*) like many waters, the
sound of their clamor (*še'on qolam, qol*) resounds" (vv. 42, 55b).[27]
This image is similar to one found in another psalm addressed to
the victorious God: "You silence the roaring (*še'on*) of the seas, the
roaring (*še'on*) of the waves, the tumult (*hamon*) of the peoples"
(65.7).[28] Thus, the *hamon* (roaring, tumult) of the waves is that
which makes up the *qol* (voice/thunder) of the sea and its *neharot*
(underwater currents). Consequently, I believe *dokyam* (from *doki*
that occurs only here in the Old Testament) is to be understood as
their pounding waves since the Hebrew *daka/dakah* has the connota-

25. Ps 24:1f; 89:25; 98:7f; Is 44:27; Jon 2:3, 5.
26. Gordon, *Ugaritic Texts* (UT), Text 68:12-25, p. 180.
27. See also Ps 89:9; Ezek 26:3.
28. See also Job 38:8, 11; Is 51:15/Jer 31:35; Zech 10:11.

tion of oppressing, pounding, crushing. This conclusion is confirmed when one reads v. 4, which resumes the thought of v. 3 by stating that the Lord is mightier than the waters and the sea waves. Indeed, in this third verse the *qolot* (voices/sounds) of the waters parallel the *mišbere yam* (the waves of the sea) in the fourth one. *mišbarim* means waves, breaking waves, sea breakers, from the Hebrew *šabar* (to break), as is clear from Ps 42:7; 88:7; 2 Sam 22:5; Jon 2:3.

V.4 Stronger than thundering waters,
Mightier than sea breakers,
Mighty in heaven is the Lord.

This verse is the second side of the diptych begun in v.3. Since the main thrust of the psalm is to declare God's victory over his enemy and God's rule over the world, v.3 can only be describing the enemy in preparation for v.4 where we read the Lord has overcome that enemy. Also, the opening of v.4 is actually a protracted comparison describing the power of the adversary while simultaneously asserting that God's power is greater.[29]

V.4c constitutes a confession of faith ("mighty in heaven is the Lord") in the same vein as the confessional statements of vv.1-2. But what is the meaning of *bammarom* (in heaven)? Technically speaking, *marom* is a high locale, a height,[30] from the verb *rum* (to be high, elevated) and refers mainly to the top of a hill or a mountain.[31] Is this the meaning of *marom* in Ps 93? Jer 31:12 and Ezek 20:24 speak of the hill of Zion where the Lord is said to be *yošeb* (sitting, seated),[32] just as the king is seated on his throne in his palace.[33] On the other

29. See also Ps. 29:3.
30. See Judg 5:18; Prov 8:2; 9:14; Jer 51:53.
31. See 2 Kings 19:23//Is 37:24; Jer 31:12; 49:16; Ezek 17:23; 20:40; 34:14.
32. See also 2 Kings 22:19; Is 6:1; Ps 9:11; 68:16; 80:1; 132:14.
33. I Kings 1 *passim*; 2:12; 3:6; 8:15; etc.; Jer 22:2, 4, 30. Note that in Hebrew the same word *hekal* means palace as well as temple, and the noun *bayit* (house) also means either the king's palace or God's temple.

hand, we also encounter passages that speak of God's being seated on a heavenly throne.[34] In two instances *šamayim* (heavens) occurs in parallel with *marom*,[35] while in Is 57:15 God says: *marom weqadoš 'eškon* (I dwell in the height, in a holy place). This suggestion of a heavenly throne and temple is made unequivocally clear in Ps 11:4 where the Hebrew *yahweh behekal qodšo yahweh baššamayim kis'o* may be translated into either: "The Lord is in his holy temple; the Lord's throne is in heaven," or "Yahweh—in the temple is his holy seat, Yahweh—in the heavens is his throne."[36] These references to Yahweh's heavenly throne sound closer to the context of Ps 93 than those referring to the hill of Zion.

V.5 Your decrees are very sure; holiness befits your house, O Lord, forevermore.

This traditional rendering of the original Hebrew presents one serious problem. It does not seem to fit the thrust of a psalm that is proclaiming the Lord's heavenly kingship. Still, I would like to mention two points in its support:

1) The shift from the celestial scene to the earthly one is not uncommon in the psalms. In Ps 24, for example, it is *human* subjects (vv. 4-6) that laud God as creator (vv. 1-2) in his holy place (v. 3b).[37] The same is true of the set of psalms 95-100 that are, like Ps 93, hymns to the Lord's kingship. In Ps 98, God's human subjects praise Him (vv. 4-6) alongside the sea and its floods (vv. 7-8). In Ps 96, these two choirs (vv. 7-9; 11b) join in with that of the gods themselves (vv. 4-5).

2) The concern with divine decrees and the priesthood of the

34. Ps 2:4; 113:5f; 123:1.
35. Ps 102:19; 148:1
36. See also Ps 29:9f.
37. Moreover, God is referred to as *'izzuz* (strong) and *gibbor* (mighty) in v. 8. Notice also the use of the same verb *nasa'* (vv. 7 and 9) as in Ps 93:3.

earthly temple reflected in the traditional rendering of v.5 occurs also in the same set of kingly psalms 95-100. In Ps 99, vv. 1-5 speak of the Lord as King and seem to introduce vv. 6-8 which mention his testimonies and statutes (v. 7). One can argue that this psalm is referring strictly to the earthly temple. The case is clearer in Ps 97 where reference to God's judgments (v. 8c) appears in a context extolling God's *celestial* kingship (vv. 1-5, 9). Again, in Ps 95, where the same kind of kingship is intended (vv. 1-5), the text exhorts human beings to hearken to the Lord's will (vv. 7c-11).

Victory and Enthronement

This study of Psalm 93 has clearly shown that the most essential attribute of kingship is victory. The king's first priority is to bring about total and sustained victory over the ultimate enemy of all who lie under his authority and responsibility. Whether the king is earthly or divine, this ultimate enemy who is always lurking about and seeking to undermine the very foundation of the kingdom's existence is typically portrayed as the adverse natural elements, especially water in the form of destructive sea waves or river flooding.[38] Nevertheless, water as potential enemy must be harnessed rather than annihilated since it is necessary for life; its absence would mean certain death for the citizens of the kingdom in the case of the earthly king or for all residents of the *tebel* (the inhabited world), in the case of God. And this is what we find described in the psalms, where threatening and potentially destructive waters are indeed harnessed, to the extent that they become an integral part of God's creation and join in the choir of all God's creatures who hail him as their king:

> O come, let us sing to the Lord;
> let us make a joyful noise to the rock of our salvation! ...

38. Powerful destructive winds, such as tornadoes, have all along been unknown in the Near East.

For the Lord is a great God,
and a great King above all gods.
In his [the Lord's] hand are the depths of the earth;
the heights of the mountains are his also.
The sea is his, for he made it;
for his hands formed the dry land. (Ps 95:1, 3-5)

Say among the nations, "The Lord reigns!
Yea, the world is established, it shall never be moved;
he will judge the peoples with equity."
Let the heavens be glad, and let the earth rejoice;
let the sea roar, and all that fills it;[39]
let the field exult, and everything in it! (Ps 96:10-12a)

Make a joyful noise to the Lord, all the earth;
break forth into joyous song and sing praises! ...
Let the sea roar, and all that fills it;
the world and all that dwell in it!
Let the floods[40] *clap their hands;*
let the hills sing for joy together
before the Lord, for he comes
to judge the earth. (Ps 98:4, 7-9a)

Hence, the victory of the king or God over the waters must be a *sustained* victory in which a potential enemy has been transformed into an actual ally. Only after the kingdom's existence was secured from disaster through fortified walls, and secured from physical want through water supply and irrigation projects—i.e., only after the king could claim permanent victory over the enemies to the kingdom's existence—could a king have a firm throne and thus be able to perform the other kingly functions.

šalom *and* simhah

This all-encompassing, permanent state of victory is composed of two essential elements: *šalom* (peace) and *simhah* (joy). The word

---

39. Notice how the originally threatening roar of the sea becomes a joyful celebration of God's victory.

40. The *neharot* in the original can also be rendered "rivers," and is the same word found thrice in Ps 93:3.

šalom designates the resulting situation after all adverse forces have been transformed into beneficent ones so that everyone in the kingdom can live an undisturbed life:

> The Lord sits enthroned over the flood;
>   the Lord sits enthroned as king for ever.
> May the Lord give strength to his people!
> May the Lord bless his people with peace! (Ps 29:10-11)

> He [God] will deliver my soul in safety (*šalom*)
>   from the battle that I wage,
>   for many are arrayed against me.
> God will give ear, and humble them,
>   he who is enthroned from old...(Ps 55:18-19a)

> In his [the king's] days may righteousness flourish,
>   and peace abound, till the moon be no more! (Ps 72:7)

> Of the increase of his government and of peace
>   there will be no end,
>   upon the throne of David, and over his kingdom,
> to establish it, and to uphold it
> with justice and with righteousness
> from this time forth and forevermore. (Is 9:7)[41]

šalom is not merely the absence of war, nor even the opposite of war (Ps 120:6-7), it is rather a post-victory—and thus post-war—situation in which the enemy has been overcome and belligerence has been annihilated. Only in this situation can one enjoy such necessities of a happy life as "friendship" and "prosperity," which explains why *šalom* is frequently translated by those words as well as by "peace":

> Even my bosom friend (*'îš šelomi*)[42] in whom I trusted,
>   who ate my bread, has lifted his heel against me. (Ps 41:9)

> My companion stretched out his hand against his friends (*bišlomayw*):[43]
>   he violated his covenant. (Ps 55:20)

> Let their own table before them become a snare;
>   let their companions[44] be a trap. (Ps 69:22)

41. See also 11:6-9 in conjunction with vv.3b-5.
42. Literally, "the man of my peace" or "my man of peace."
43. The word *šalom* is in the plural here.
44. The RSV translates "sacrificial feasts," following the Targum; but the original Hebrew has the same word as in Ps 55:20 (*šalom* in the plural).

> But the meek shall possess the land,
>> and delight themselves in abundant prosperity (*šalom*). (Ps 37:11)

The *šalom* established by an earthly king, the heavenly king, or both working together serves as the foundation for *simhah* (joy, gladness, exultation), and that is why the latter word appears frequently in conjunction with mention of kingship,[45] the throne,[46] and the king's residence.[47]

---

45. See Ps 5:2 and 11; 21:1, 6; 63:11; 86:4; 96:10-11; 97:1, 8, 11-12; 149:2.
46. See Ps 9:2 and 7; 33:14 and 21.
47. See Ps 33:14 and 21; Ps 45:15. Many refer to the sanctuary ("Zion," "temple," "tabernacle," etc.) as God's dwelling place: Ps 14:7; 43:3-4; 46:4; 48:11; 53:6; 68:3 and 5; 100:2 and 4; 118:24 and 26-27; 122:1; 126:1 and 3; 137:6.

3

The Other Kingly Functions

Subjection of Human Enemies

In the Ancient Near East—as is still true today—any people's peace and well-being requires control not only of the adverse powers of nature but also of human adversaries. In order to remain on the throne, a king must be victorious over other kings who lead their nations in battle against him and his city. As for the heavenly king, God's natural adversaries would be the other gods, but since his realm, the *tebel* (inhabited world) is specially represented by his own city where he reigns in the temple built in his honor, the earthly enemies of that city are also his enemies. Therefore the psalms depict God as victorious over both human and (supposedly) divine adversaries:

> O sing to the Lord a new song;
>> sing to the Lord, all the earth!
>> Sing to the Lord, bless his name;
>> tell of his salvation from day to day.
>> Declare his glory among the nations,
>> his marvelous works among the peoples!
>> For great is the Lord, and greatly to be praised;
>> he is to be feared above all gods.
>> For all the gods of the peoples are idols;
>> but the Lord made the heavens. (Ps 96:1-5)

> The heavens proclaim his righteousness;
>> and all the peoples behold his glory.
>> All worshipers of images are put to shame,
>> who make their boast in worthless idols;
>> all gods bow down before him ...

> For Thou, O Lord, are most high over all the earth;
>> thou art exalted far above all gods. (Ps 97:7, 9)

> The Lord has made known his victory,
>> he has revealed his vindication in the sight of the nations. (Ps 98:2)

The Lord reigns; let the people tremble!
>He sits enthroned upon the cherubim; let the earth quake!
>The Lord is great in Zion;
>he is exalted over all the peoples. (Ps 99:1-2)

For lo, the kings assembled,
>they came on together.
>As soon as they saw it, they were astounded,
>they were in panic, they took to flight;
>trembling took hold of them there,
>anguish as a woman in travail. (Ps 48:4-6)[1]

And here again, as in the case of the destructive waters, the defeated enemies are not annihilated but rather subdued and forced to join in the choir of the inhabitants of God's city:

Ascribe to the Lord, O families of the peoples,
>ascribe to the Lord glory and strength! (Ps 96:7)

All the ends of the earth shall remember
>and turn to the Lord;
>and all the families of the nations
>shall worship before him. (Ps 22:27)

Ascribe to the Lord, O heavenly beings,[2]
>ascribe to the Lord glory and strength. (Ps 29:1)

Clap your hands, all peoples!
>Shout to God with loud songs of joy!...
>God reigns over the nations;
>God sits on his holy throne.
>The princes of the peoples gather
>as the people of the God of Abraham.[3] (Ps 47:1, 8-9a)

Bless our God, O peoples,
>let the sound of his praise be heard. (Ps 66:8)

Let the peoples praise thee, O God;
>let the peoples praise thee! (Ps 67: 3 and 5)

There is none like thee among the gods, O Lord,
>nor are there any works like thine.

1. See also Ps 47:3, 8.
2. *bene 'elim* in the original, which means "sons of gods."
3. Or as Dahood, I:281, renders v.9a: "O nobles of the peoples, gather round! The God of Abraham is the Strong One."

> All the nations thou hast made shall come
>   and bow down before thee, O Lord,
>   and shall glorify thy name. (Ps 86:8-9)

Praise the Lord, all nations!
>   Extol him, all peoples! (Ps 117:1)

This does not mean the other gods, kings, and foreign nations have once and for all put aside any attempt at overthrowing God's suzerainty over them. Like the chaotic waters and like any vassal, they keep threatening to do just that and God must continuously maintain his sovereignty over them:

> Why do the nations conspire,
>   and the peoples plot in vain?
>   The kings of the earth set themselves,
>   and the rulers take counsel together,
>   against the Lord and his anointed, saying,
>   "Let us burst their bonds asunder,
>   and cast their cords from us." (Ps 2:1-3)

> There did we rejoice in him,
>   who rules by his might for ever,
>   whose eyes keep watch on the nations—
>   let not the rebellious exalt themselves. (Ps 66:7)

> O God, do not keep silence;
>   do not hold thy peace or be still, O God!
>   For lo, thy enemies are in tumult;
>   those who hate thee have raised their heads.
>   They lay crafty plans against thy people;
>   they consult together against thy protected ones.
>   They say, "Come, let us wipe them out as a nation;
>   let the name of Israel be remembered no more!"
>   Yea, they conspire in one accord;
>   against thee they make a covenant—
>   the tents of Edom and the Ishmaelites,
>   Moab and the Hagrites,
>   Gebal and Ammon and Amalek,
>   Philistia with the inhabitants of Tyre;
>   Assyria has joined them;
>   they are the strong arm of the children of Lot. (Ps 83:1-8)

Justice

The throne of victory is at the same time a throne of justice. It is not enough merely to defeat and contain the enemy; the ensuing state of victory must also be one in which equitable judgment rules the affairs of the victorious people. This is crystal clear from the passages where notions of victory (or enthronement) and justice are mentioned in parallel. A few examples:

> Say among the nations, "The Lord reigns!"
>> Yea, the world is established, it shall never be moved;
>> he will judge (*yadin*) the peoples with equity...
>> for he comes to judge (*lišpot, špt*) the earth.
>> He will judge (*yišpot, špt*) the earth with righteousness,
>> and the peoples with his truth. (Ps 96:10, 13)
>
> But the Lord sits enthroned for ever,
>> he has established his throne for judgment (*lammišpat, špt*);
>> and he judges (*yišpot, špt*) the world with righteousness,
>> he judges (*yadin*) the peoples with equity. (Ps 9:7-8)[4]

However, the function of judgment is not of secondary importance after victory; indeed, the divine throne is essentially a seat of judgment. When God is seated on his throne as the supreme deity among the gods, it seems his basic function is to judge among the other gods themselves!

> God has taken his place in the divine council;
>> in the midst of the gods he holds judgment (*yišpot, špt*):
>> "How long will you judge (*tišpetu, špt*) unjustly
>> and show partiality to the wicked?[5]
>> Give justice (*šiptu, špt*) to the weak and the fatherless;
>> maintain the right of the afflicted and the destitute.
>> Rescue the weak and needy;
>> deliver them from the hands of the wicked."
>> They have neither knowledge nor understanding,
>> they walk about in darkness;
>> all the foundations of the earth are shaken.
>> I say, "You are gods,

4. See also Ps 98:9.
5. See also Ps 58:1-2.

sons of the Most High, all of you;
nevertheless, you shall die like men,
and fall like any prince."
Arise, O God, judge (*šoptah, špt*) the earth;
for to thee belong all the nations! (Ps 82)

That the throne functions as a seat of judgment should come as
no surprise to the reader of the Old Testament. Both the Deuteronomistic Historian and the Chronicler depict Solomon as the king par
excellence:[6] He entered into a marriage alliance with Pharaoh, the
greatest ruler in the Near East at that time (1 Kg 3:1); in him lay the
fullness of kingly wisdom (1 Kg 3:4-15//2 Chr 1:3-12); he is the only
king for whom we are given a complete list of the high officials of his
kingdom (1 Kg 4); he was the builder of the Jerusalem temple and
palace (1 Kg 5:15-7:51//2 Chr 2:1-5:1); he was the high priest
praying and sacrificing to God on behalf of the people at the conse-
cration of the temple (1 Kg 8//2 Chr 5:2-7:10); his richness and
power were great and his fame was far-reaching (1 Kg 9:26-10:29//2
Chr 8:17-9:28). Yet, both accounts begin their story with an introductory chapter where Solomon is tested by God; all his future
greatness would come to pass only if he could wisely answer a
question concerning his own understanding of his role as king. To the
question, "Ask what I shall give you,"[7] (1 Kg 3:5//2 Chr 1:7) Solomon replied:

> ...And now, O Lord my God, thou hast made thy servant king in place of
> David my father, although I am but a little child; I do not know how to
> go out or come in. And thy servant is in the midst of thy people whom
> thou hast chosen, a great people, that cannot be numbered or counted for
> multitude. Give thy servant therefore an understanding mind to govern
> (*lišpot, špt*) thy people, that I may discern between good and evil; for who
> is able to govern (*lišpot, špt*) thy great people? (1 Kg 3:7-9)

> ...O Lord God, let thy promise to David my father be now fulfilled, for thou
> hast made me king over a people as many as the dust of the earth. Give me

6. The Chronicler introduces his report on the Solomonic reign by writing: "Solomon
the son of David established himself in his kingdom, and the Lord his God was with
him and made him exceedingly great." (2 Chr 1:1)
7. That is, "Ask what you would want me to give you."

now wisdom and knowledge to go out and come in before this people, for who can rule (*yišpot, špt*) this thy people, that is so great? (1 Chr 1:9-10)

In the Deuteronomistic History this is followed by the famous story where Solomon judges between the two women and the baby (1 Kg 3:16-28), and after this, "... all Israel heard of the judgment (*mišpat, špt*) which the king had rendered; and they stood in awe of the king, because they perceived that the wisdom of God was in him, to render justice (*mišpat, špt*)." Whether translated "judge," "govern," or "rule," this function is not merely a welcome addition to the kingly throne but rather an essential part of it:

Give the king thy justice (*mišpateka, špt*)
and thy righteousness (*sidqateka, sdq*) to the royal son!
May he judge (*yadin*) thy people with righteousness (*sedeq, sdq*)
and thy poor with justice (*bemišpat, špt*)! (Ps 72:1-2)

It is an abomination to kings to do evil,
for the throne is established (*yikkon, kun*) by righteousness (*bisdaqah, sdq*). (Prov 16:12)

Take away the dross from the silver,
and the smith has material for a vessel;
take away the wicked from the presence of the king,
and his throne is established (*weyikkon, kun*) in righteousness (*bassedeq, sdq*). (Prov 25:4-5)

If a king judges (*šopet, špt*) the poor with equity (*be'emet, 'mt*)
his throne will be established (*yikkon, kun*) for ever. (Prov 29:14)

Of the increase of his government and of peace
there will be no end,
upon the throne of David, and over his kingdom,
to establish (*lehakin, kun*) it, and to uphold it
with justice (*bemišpat, špt*) and with righteousness (*ubisdaqah, sdq*)
from this time forth and forevermore. (Is 9:7)[8]

The first of these is from the psalm quoted in ch.1 to show that the person of the king was understood to be the source and sustainer of all life. And the others use the verb *nakon* (to be established, *kun*) in a manner similar to that of Ps 93,[9] where both the world and the

8. See also Is 11:3b-5.
9. See above.

divine throne are established. These similarities reflect an under-standing that without kingly justice no king or kingdom can last; and by the same token, without divine justice the deity itself and the world itself are in danger. That this is true of the divine world as well as the human one can be seen in Ps 82. If "the gods" (v.1) will judge unjustly or fail to render justice to the poor and downtrodden (v.2-4),[10] "the foundations of the earth will be shaken" (v.5), and they themselves, in spite of their divine status (v.6), will be called into judgment and will perish as if they were human princes (v.7)![11]

The Wicked

A thorough implementation of justice demands not merely the defense of the wronged but also the punishment of the wrong-doer and the eradication of evil:

> On the wicked (*rešaʿim, ršʿ*) he [God] will rain coal of fire and brimstone;
> a scorching wind shall be the portion of their cup. (Ps 11:6)

> A king who sits in the throne of judgment
> winnows all evil (*raʿ, rʿ*) with his eyes. (Prov 20:8)

> A wise king winnows the wicked (*rešaʿim, ršʿ*),
> and drives the wheel over them. (Prov 20:26)

> He shall not judge by what his eyes see,
> or decide by what his ears hear;
> but with righteousness he shall judge the poor,
> and decide with equity for the meek of the earth;
> and he shall smite the earth with the rod of his mouth,
> and with the breath of his lips he shall slay all the wicked (*rašaʿ, ršʿ*)
> (Is 11:3b-4)

The seriousness of the matter has to do with the fact that *raʿ* (evil, *rʿ*) and *rašaʿ* (*ršʿ*) in the general sense of "wickedness" threaten the throne itself and thus the very existence of the

10. See also Ps 72:2, 3, 12-14.
11. Even the gods answer to God for their behavior toward the kingdoms assigned to their care by Him. He is "feared in the council of the holy ones, great and terrible above all that are around him." (Ps 89:7)

kingdom. This is because both are ultimately expressions of *peša'*
(*pš'*) in the narrower sense of "rebellion," an action deserving
nothing less than capital punishment:[12]

> But transgressors (*poše'im, pš'*) shall be altogether destroyed;
>> the posterity of the wicked (*reša'im, rš'*) shall be cut off. (Ps 37:38)

> For thou art not a God who delights in wickedness (*peša', pš'*);
>> evil (*ra', r'*) may not sojourn with thee ...
>> Make them bear their guilt, O God;
>> let them fall by their own counsels;
>> because of their many transgressions (*piš'ehem, pš'*) cast them out
>> for they have rebelled against thee. (Ps 5:4, 10)

Closely related to the "rebellion" of a king's own subjects is the
aggression of enemies. Be they neighboring kingdoms or the
destructive forces of nature, their harmful work is also considered
"wickedness" and "evildoing":

> Arise, O Lord, in thy anger,
>> lift thyself up against the fury of my enemies;
>> awake, O my God, thou hast appointed a judgment.
>> Let the assembly of the peoples be gathered about thee;
>> and over it take thy seat on high.
>> The Lord judges the peoples;
>> judge me, O Lord, according to my righteousness
>> and according to the integrity that is in me.
>> O let the evil (*ra', r'*) of the wicked (*reša'im, rš'*) come to an end,
>> but establish thou the righteous,
>> thou who triest the minds and hearts,
>> thou righteous God. (Ps 7:6-9)[13]

> Thou hast rebuked the nations, thou hast destroyed the wicked;
>> thou hast blotted out their name for ever and ever...
>> The nations have sunk in the pit which they made;
>> in the net which they hid has their own foot been caught.
>> the Lord has made himself known, he has executed judgment;
>> the wicked are snared in the work of their hands.
>> The wicked shall depart to Sheol,
>> all the nations that forget God. (Ps 9:5, 15-16)

12. See comments on *peša'* in vol.2, pp.32-33, 42, 52.
13. See also Ps 3:1-2, 7.

Break thou the arm of the wicked and the evildoer;
seek out his wickedness till thou find none.
The Lord is king for ever and ever;
the nations shall perish from his land. (Ps 10:15-16)

Let God arise, let his enemies be scattered;
let those who hate him flee before him!
As smoke is driven away, so drive them away;
as wax melts before fire,
let the wicked perish before God! (Ps 68:1-2)

I call upon the Lord, who is worthy to be praised,
and I am saved from my enemies.
The cords of death encompassed me,
the torrents of perdition assailed me...
He reached from on high, he took me,
he drew me out of many waters.
He delivered me from my strong enemy,
and from those who hated me...
For I have kept the ways of the Lord,
and have not wickedly departed from my God. (Ps 18:3-4, 16-17, 21)

Nevertheless, the enemies without are less dangerous than the enemies within, "wolves in sheep's clothing" who strike without warning. These are an ever-present danger, daily assailing the throne through plots or bribes.[14] The most difficult struggle for a king or deity is against unfaithful insiders, the "enemies" par excellence who are deadlier than foreign rulers and adverse natural phenomena. As we shall see later, the king will beseech his God to save him particularly from the wicked and evil ones that surround him.

Universalism Versus Locality

The "universal" aspect of a monarch's rule (his power over foreign kings and nations) goes hand in hand with the "local" aspect (his rule over his own subjects) as an equal and essential component of the definition of kingship. To be master over nations threatening his kingdom a king must first have his own realm under control, and

14. See Ps 26:5, 10; Prov 17:23; Is 5:23 (The RSV "guilty" is the rendering of an original *raša'* [wicked]).

in order to retain control of his own realm he must be able to eventually subjugate the surrounding kings and their nations: the *one* throne must perform *both functions*. The same applies to the deity, who may be considered to have universal authority but nevertheless must have a "home base." Hence the *necessity* of a given mountain or shrine for a deity to rule over the world.[15] Just as a king or even an emperor was known as the monarch of a city,[16] a deity was defined by its temple, located either on a (comparatively high) mountain[17] or in a city.[18] Without some such frame of reference it would be impossible to conceive of any deity, and thus only a localized deity could rule or exist as a universal deity.

One reflection of this understanding may be seen in the way a god would be presented as *going forth* from its mountain just as a king would *go forth* from his city. Even Yahweh, who for nascent Judaism was understood to be the sole, universal God,[19] "went forth" from his earthly home:

> The Lord came from Sinai,
> > and dawned from Seir upon us;
> > he shone forth from Mount Paran...(Deut 33:2a)
> Lord, when thou didst go forth from Seir,
> > when thou didst march from the region of Edom...(Judg 5:4a)
> God came from Teman,
> > and the Holy One from Mount Paran. (Hab 3:3)

The importance of the link between the deity and a mountain can also be seen in the fact that the term *sur*, meaning rock, and consequently mountain or fortress, became a major epithet for God himself.[20] It is also reflected in the way the deity's city was viewed cultically as being its "mountain," with the consequence that "God's temple," even when the

15. See comments on Ps 93:2 above.
16. For example, the Egyptian Pharaoh was the king of Memphis or Thebes; the Assyrian emperor was the king of Niniveh; the Persian emperor was the king of Persepolis. In the case of the Babylonian and Roman hegemonies, it was the royal city—Babylon and Rome, respectively—that lent its name to the entire empire!
17. As in the case of *ba'al sapon*, Baal of (Mount) Zaphon, and Zeus of (Mount) Olympus.
18. As in the case of Yahweh of Zion/Jerusalem and Apollo of Delphi.
19. See vol.1, pp.121-126.
20. Ps 18:2, 31; 19:14; 28:1; 31:3; 62:2, 6, 7; 71:3; 73:26 (RSV has "strength" for the same Hebrew word *sur*); 78:35; 89:26; 92:15; 94:22; 95:1; 144:1.

term occurs in conjunction with Zion, could refer to either location in the mind of the psalmist. Consider the following instances:

> The Lord is my rock, and my fortress, and my deliverer,
>> my God, my rock (*my mountain*, [*suri*, *sur*]), in whom I take refuge,
>> my shield, and the horn of my salvation, my stronghold.
> In my distress I called upon the Lord;
> to my God I cried for help.
> From *his temple* he heard my voice,
> and my cry to him reached his ears. (Ps 18: 2, 6)

> The Lord is my light and my salvation;
>> whom shall I fear?
>> The Lord is the stronghold of my life;[21]
>> of whom shall I be afraid? ...
>> One thing have I asked of the Lord ...
>> that I may dwell in *the house of the Lord*
>> all the days of my life,
>> to behold the beauty of the Lord,
>> and to inquire in *his temple*.
>> For he will hide me in his shelter in the day of trouble;
>> he will conceal me under the cover of *his tent*,
>> he will set me high *upon a rock* (*besur*, *sur*). (Ps 27:1, 4-5)

> Great is the Lord and greatly to be praised
>> in *the city* of our God!
>> *His holy mountain*, beautiful in elevation,
>> is the joy of the *all the earth*,[22]
>> *Mount Zion*, in the far north,[23]
>> *the city* of the great King.
>> *Within her citadels* God
>> has shown himself a sure defense...
>> We have thought on thy steadfast love, O God,
>> in the midst of *thy temple*.
>> As thy name, O God,
>> so thy praise reaches to *the ends of the earth*.
>> Thy right hand is filled with victory;
>> let *Mount Zion* be glad! (Ps 48:1-3, 9-10)

21. Compare to Ps 18:2c.
22. See Lam 2:15.
23. Here Zion is compared to the high mountain Zaphon.

Sing to God, sing praises to his holy name;
    lift up a song to him *who rides upon the clouds...*
    Father of the fatherless and protector of widows
    is God in *his holy habitation...*
    Thou didst *ascend the high mount,*
    leading captives in thy train,
    and receiving gifts among men...
    Because of *thy temple at Jerusalem*
    kings bring gifts to thee...
    Sing to God, O kingdoms of the earth;
    sing praises to the Lord,
    to him *who rides in the heavens, the ancient heavens;*
    lo, he sends forth his voice, his mighty voice.
    Ascribe power to God,
    whose majesty is *over Israel,*
    and his power is *in the skies.*
    Terrible is God *in his sanctuary...* (Ps 68:4, 5, 18, 29, 32-35)

For all the gods of the peoples are idols;
    but the Lord made *the heavens.*
    Honor and majesty are before him;
    strength and beauty are *his sanctuary.* (Ps 96:5-6)

It is no wonder then that Mount Zion (Jerusalem), which in reality is a mere rocky protrusion less elevated than the nearby Mount of Olives, is transformed in the cult into a mountain of unique beauty and height:

His [God's] holy mountain, beautiful in elevation,
    is the joy of the all the earth,
    Mount Zion, in the far north,
    the city of the great King. (Ps 48:1c-2)

Out of Zion, the perfection of beauty, God shines forth. (Ps 50:2)

It shall come to pass in the latter days
    that the mountain of the house of the Lord
    shall be established as the highest of the mountains,
    and shall be raised above the hills... (Is 2:2//Mic 4:1)

4

God's Kingly Attributes

Loyalty and Faithfulness (hesed we'emet)

Loyalty and faithfulness (*hesed we'emet*) preserve the king,
and his throne is upheld by righteousness.[1] (Prov 20:28)

Prolong the life of the king;
may his years endure to all generations!
May he be enthroned forever before God;
bid steadfast love and faithfulness (*hesed we'emet*) watch over him!
(Ps 61:6-7)

The twins *hesed* and *'emet* are the backbone of kingship and thus
of the entire kingdom.[2] They support the king in his struggle
against evil, his primary enemy: "Do they not err that devise evil
(*ra'*)? Those who devise good meet loyalty (*hesed*) and faithfulness (*'emet*) " (Prov 14:22) And it is precisely these twin attributes
that the psalms often ascribe to God.[3] They are considered not
mere personal virtues but essential assets of the divine throne (identified by words such as "temple," "heavens," or "clouds" as well as
"throne") and are thus an integral part of the very definition of what
it means to be a god:

He [God] will send down from heaven and save me,
he will put to shame those who trample upon me.
God will send forth his steadfast love and his faithfulness (*hasdo
wa'amitto*, **hesed we'emet**)! ...
For thy steadfast love (*hasdeka, hesed*) is great to the heavens,
thy faithfulness (*'amitteka, 'emet*) to the clouds. (Ps 57:3, 10)

1. The RSV follows here the Septuagint which has *dikaiosyne* (righteousness) whereas
the Hebrew reads *hesed* (faithfulness), repeating what is found in the first half of the
verse.
2. See Prov 3:3; 16:6.
3. Ps 25:10; 26:3; 40:11; 69:13; 86:15; 115:1; 138:2.

For thy steadfast love (*hasdeka,* **hesed**) is great above the heavens,
  thy faithfulness (*'amitteka, 'emet*) reaches the clouds. (Ps 108:4)
I will sing of thy steadfast love O Lord (*hasde* [**hesed**] *yahweh*), for ever;
  with my mouth I will proclaim thy faithfulness (*'emunateka, 'mnh*)[4]
  to all generations.
For thy steadfast love (*hasdeka,* **hesed**) was established for ever,
  thy faithfulness (*'emunateka, 'mnh*) is firm as the heavens.
Righteousness and justice are the foundation of thy throne;
  steadfast love and faithfulness (*hesed we'emet*) go before thee.
Ps 89:1-2, 14)

I bow down toward thy holy temple and give thanks to thy name
  for thy steadfast love (*hasdeka,* **hesed**) and thy faithfulness (*'amitteka,
  'emet*). (Ps 138:2a)

...who [God] made heaven and earth,
  the sea, and all that is in them;
  who keeps faith (*'emet*) for ever; (Ps 146:6)

It is no wonder then that the refrain of each of the 26 verses of
Psalm 136 is: "for his steadfast love (*hasdo,* **hesed**) endures for
ever," and that the shortest psalm reads:

Praise the Lord all nations!
  Extol him, all peoples!
  For great is his steadfast love (*hasdo,* **hesed**) toward us;
  and the faithfulness (*'emet*) of the Lord endures for ever.
  Praise the Lord! (Ps 117)

Since *hesed* is a central attribute of the deity, one frequently
finds the word's adjectival form (*hasid,* often "loyal" or "godly" in
RSV)[5] and verbal form (*yithassed* [**hsd**]—often "show oneself to
be loyal") associated with God. He is the *hasid* par excellence; his
hesed is "blameless" (*tam*) or perfect, and it is manifested in
myriad concrete actions:

The Lord is just in all his ways,
  and kind (*hasid*) in all his doings. (Ps 145:17)
I will not look on you in anger,
  for I am merciful (*hasid*), says the Lord. (Jer 3:12)

4. From the same root as *'emet.*

5. See examples of the latter in Deut 33:8; Ps 43:1 (ungodly translates *lo' hasid,* i.e., not
godly); 52:11; 86:2.

With the loyal (*hasid*) thou dost show thyself loyal (*tithassad, hsd*);
    with the blameless (*tamim,* **tam**) man thou dost show thyself blame-
    less (*tittammam,* **tam**) ...
This God—his way is perfect (*tamim,* **tam**);
    the promise of the Lord proves true;
    he is a shield for those who take refuge in him. (Ps 18:25, 30)

Let them thank the Lord for his steadfast love (*hasdo,* **hesed**),
    for his wonderful works to the sons of men!
For he satisfies him who is thirsty,
    and the hungry he fills with good things ...
he brought them out of darkness and gloom,
    and broke their bonds asunder.
Let them thank the Lord for his steadfast love (*hasdo,* **hesed**),
    for his wonderful works to the sons of men!
For he shatters the doors of bronze,
    and cuts in two the bars of iron ...
he sent forth his word, and healed them,
    and delivered them from destruction.
 Let them thank the Lord for his steadfast love (*hasdo,* **hesed**),
    for his wonderful works to the sons of men!
And let them offer sacrifices of thanksgiving,
    and tell of his deeds in songs of joy! (Ps 107: 8-9, 14-16, 20-22)

God's Righteousness

God's basic attribute being justice,[6] his *hesed,* which is loyalty,
faithfulness, love, and care, must go hand in hand with *sedaqah* or
sedeq (righteousness):

Steadfast love (*hesed*) and faithfulness will meet;
    righteousness (*sedeq*) and peace will kiss each other. (Ps 85:10)

Righteousness (*sedeq*) and justice are the foundation of thy throne;
    steadfast love (*hesed*) and faithfulness go before thee. (Ps 89:14)[7]

But I through the abundance of thy steadfast love (*hasdeka,* **hesed**) will
    enter thy house...
    Lead me, O Lord, in thy righteousness (*sidqateka, sedaqah*) (Ps 5:7, 8)

6. See ch.3
7. See also Ps 97:2.

He [the Lord] loves righteousness (*sedaqah*) and justice;
   the earth is full of the steadfast love (*hesed*) of the Lord (Ps 33:5)

Thy steadfast love (*hasdeka,* **hesed**), O Lord, extends to the heavens,
   thy faithfulness to the clouds.
   Thy righteousness (*sidqateka, sedaqah*) is like the mountains of God,
   thy judgments are like the great deep ...
   O continue thy loving kindness (*hasdeka,* **hesed**) to those who know
   thee,
   and thy salvation (*sidqateka, sedaqah*) to the upright of heart! (Ps
   36:5-6, 10)

But the steadfast love (*hesed*) of the Lord is from everlasting to everlasting
   upon those who fear him,
   and his righteousness (*sidqato, sedaqah*) to children's children...
   (Ps 103:17)

In thy righteousness (*sidqateka, sedaqah*) bring me out of trouble!
   And in thy steadfast love (*hasdeka,* **hesed**) cut off my enemies...(Ps
   143:11b-12a)

Like God's *hesed,* his righteousness "reaches the high heavens" (Ps
71:19) and "looks down from the sky" (Ps 85:11b), and the
divine throne itself is a seat of righteousness:

...thou hast sat on the throne giving righteous judgment (*šopet* [*špt*]
   sedeq)...
   But the Lord sits enthroned forever,
   he has established his throne for judgment;
   and he judges the world with righteousness (*besedeq,* **sedeq**),
   he judges the peoples with equity. (Ps 9:4b, 7-8)

...for he [the Lord] comes to judge the earth.
   He will judge the world with righteousness (*besedeq,* **sedeq**),
   and the peoples with his truth. (Ps 96:13//98:9)

The Lord reigns; let the people tremble!
   He sits enthroned upon the cherubim; let the earth quake!...
   Mighty King, lover of justice,
   thou hast established equity;
   thou hast executed justice
   and righteousness (*sedaqah*) in Jacob. (Ps 99:1, 4)

The parallelism between *hesed* and *sedeq/sedaqah* is not merely
a poetic convention but reflects a real similarity in meaning

between the two. The Semitic root *sdq* does not just mean uprightness or correctness in the sense of sound and just judgment (*mišpat*). It also can be synonymous with *hesed*, having the same connotations of grace, kindness, generosity, and benevolence. The clearest possible instance of *sedaqah* meaning "generosity" or "gift" occurs in Joel 2:23:

> Be glad, O sons of Zion,
>> and rejoice in the Lord, your God;
>> for he has given the early rain for your vindication (*lisdaqah, sedaqah*),
>> he has poured down for you abundant rain,
>> the early and the latter rain, as before.

The RSV rendering "for your vindication" makes no sense in the immediate context which speaks of the gift of rain, especially in the larger context of ch.3: after having punished his people by sending locusts over their land (vv.1-11) and calling for their repentance (vv.12-17), "the Lord became jealous for his land, and had pity on his people" (v.18) and restored the land's plenty (vv.19-22, 24-27) through his gift of rain (v.23). Hence, the only possible meaning of *lisdaqah* in 2:23 is "for (as) a gift; as an act of generosity/benevolence (on the Lord's part),"[8] and consequently "in abundance."

When we turn to the Psalms, we encounter a similar use of *sedeq* and *sedaqah* with their connotation of benevolence and generosity, expressed through good deeds. A good starting point is Ps 85, where parallel reference is made to both *hesed* and *sedeq*:

> Lord, thou wast favorable to thy land;
>> thou didst restore the fortunes of Jacob.
>> Thou didst forgive the iniquity of thy people;
>> thou didst pardon all their sin.
>> Thou didst withdraw all thy wrath;
>> thou didst turn from thy hot anger.

8. Note also that the RSV has added, before "vindication," the possessive adjective "your" which is not in the original Hebrew. And there is no other place in Joel where this word carries a different meaning; except for 2:23, no other form of the root *sdq* occurs anywhere at all in Joel.

> Restore us again, O God of our salvation...
> Show us thy steadfast love (*hasdeka*, **hesed**), O Lord,
> and grant us thy salvation.
> Let me hear what God the Lord will speak,
> for he will speak peace to his people,
> to his saints (*hasidayw*, **hasid**),[9] to those who turn to him in their hearts.
> Surely his salvation is at hand for those who fear him,
> that glory may dwell in our land.
> Steadfast love and faithfulness (*hesed we'emet*) will meet;
> righteousness (*sedeq*) and peace will kiss each other.
> Faithfulness will spring up from the ground
> and righteousness (*sedeq*) will look down from the sky.
> Yea, the Lord will give what is good,
> and our land will yield its increase.
> Righteousness (*sedeq*) will go before him,
> and make his footsteps a way. (vv.1-4a, 7-13)

Furthermore, in the text just quoted, the Lord's *hesed* is mentioned in v.7 in conjunction with *yeša'* (salvation), which is an action done by him on behalf of his people; hence his title "God of our salvation" (v.4a). In its turn, the Lord's salvation occurs as a counterpart to his *sedaqah*:

> Shower, O heavens, from above,
>> and let the skies rain down righteousness (*sedeq*);
> let the earth open, that salvation may sprout forth,
>> and let it cause righteousness (*sedaqah*) to spring up also;
> I the Lord have created it. (Is 45:8)

> Thus says the Lord:
>> "Keep justice and do righteousness
> for soon my salvation will come,
>> and my deliverance (*sidqati*, *sedaqah*) be revealed." (Is 56:1)

> "It is I, announcing vindication (*sedaqah*),
>> mighty to save." (Is 63:1c)

In Ps 111, the Lord's righteousness parallels his good deeds:

> Great are the works of the Lord,
>> studied by all who have pleasure in them.

---

9. The recipients of God's *hesed* are referred to as *hasidim*, the plural of *hasid*, which is a qualifier of God himself as the grantor of *hesed* (see above).

Full of honor and majesty is his work,
and his righteousness (*sidqato, sedaqah*) endures for ever ...
He provides food for those who fear him;
he is ever mindful of his covenant.
He has shown his people the power of his works,
in giving them the heritage of the nations.
The works of his hands are faithful and just;
all his precepts are trustworthy. (vv.2-3, 5-7)

The link to "good deeds" is similarly apparent in Ps 71:

In thy righteousness (*besidqateka, sedaqah*) deliver me and rescue me;
incline thy ear to me, and save me! ...
Rescue me, O my God, from the hand of the wicked,
from the grasp of the unjust and cruel man ...
My mouth will tell of thy righteous acts (*sidqateka, sedaqah*),
of thy deeds of salvation all the day,
for their number is past my knowledge.
With the mighty deeds of the Lord God I will come,
I will praise thy righteousness (*sidqateka, sedaqah*), thine alone.
O God, from my youth thou hast taught me,
and I still proclaim thy wondrous deeds ...[10]
And my tongue will talk of thy righteous help (*sidqateka, sedaqah*)
all the day long,
for they have been put to shame and disgraced
who sought to do me hurt. (Ps 71:2, 4, 15-17, 24)

The idea that God's righteousness is expressed through specific "acts" that can be numbered is so clearly expressed in v.15 that the RSV renders *sedaqah* with "righteous acts" (v.15),[11] and because of the persistent theme of "rescue from evil aggression" the same word is rendered "righteous help" in v.24. The emphasis on deeds as opposed to abstract qualities can also be seen in the divine appellation "Thou who hast done great things" (v.19) and in the use of *geburot* (v.16), plural of *geburah* (power/might, v.18), to speak of the Lord's "mighty deeds." Finally, Psalm 145 offers an instance where *sedaqah* refers both to God's benevolence/goodness and his deeds:

10. The original Hebrew for "wondrous deeds" here is *niple'ot*, the same word rendered as "wonderful works" in Ps 107 quoted above where it refers to the Lord's *hesed*.

11. "Salvation" (*tešu'ah*) is similarly expanded into "deeds of salvation" in the same verse.

One generation shall laud thy works to another,
    and shall declare thy mighty acts.
On the glorious splendor of thy majesty,
    and on thy wondrous works, I will meditate.
Men shall proclaim the might of thy terrible acts,
    and I will declare thy greatness.
They shall pour forth the fame of thy abundant goodness,
    and shall sing aloud of thy righteousness (*sidqateka, sedaqah*).
(Ps 145:4-7)

All the preceding explains the frequent reference to God as *saddiq* in parallel with *hasid* in general and with his acts of benevolence in particular:

O Lord my God, in thee do I take refuge;
    save me from all my pursuers, and deliver me...
    O let the evil of the wicked come to an end,
    but establish thou the righteous,
    thou who triest the minds and hearts,
    thou righteous (*saddiq*) God.
    My shield is with God,
    who saves the upright in heart,
    God is a righteous (*saddiq*) judge,
    and a God who has indignation every day. (Ps 7:1, 9-11)

In the Lord I take refuge;
    how can you say to me,
    "Flee like a bird to the mountains;
    for lo, the wicked bend the bow,
    they have fitted their arrow to the string,
    to shoot in the dark at the upright in heart;
    if the foundations are destroyed,
    what can the righteous (*saddiq*) do"? ...
    On the wicked he will rain coals of fire and brimstone;
    a scorching wind shall be the portion of their cup.
    For the Lord is righteous (*saddiq*), he loves righteous deeds (*sedaqot, sedaqah*);
    the upright shall behold his face. (Ps 11:1-3, 6-7)

The Lord is righteous (*saddiq*);
    he has cut the cords of the wicked. (Ps 129:4)

The Lord upholds all who are falling,

and raises up all who are bowed down.
The eyes of all look to thee,
and thou gavest them their food in due season.
Thou openest thy hand,
thou satisfiest the desire of every living thing.
The Lord is just (*saddiq*) in all his ways,
and kind (*hasid*) in all his doings. (Ps 145:14-17)

I love the Lord, because he has heard
my voice and my supplications...
Gracious is the Lord, and righteous (*saddiq*);
our God is merciful.
The Lord preserves the simple;
when I was brought low, he saved me.
Return, O my soul, to your rest;
for the Lord has dealt bountifully with you. (Ps 116:1, 5-7)

The last passage associates *saddiq* with "gracious" (*hannun*) and
"merciful" (*merahem, rhm*), as does Ps 112: "The Lord is gracious
(*hannun*), merciful (*rahum, rhm*), and righteous (*saddiq*)." The
same is true of Ps 111 quoted above, where righteousness is
paralleled with benevolent deeds: "Full of honor and majesty is his
work, and his righteousness (*sidqato, sedaqah*) endures for ever.
He has caused his wonderful works to be remembered; the Lord
is gracious (*hannun*) and merciful (*rahum, rhm*)."

God's glory

Glory (*kabod*) is another royal attribute that became a quintessentially
divine one; the Psalms frequently speak of God's glory and occasionally
associate that glory either with his title of "king" or with words expressing related concepts such as "kingdom," "reign," or "throne":

Declare his glory among the nations ...
Ascribe to the Lord, O families of the earth,
ascribe to the Lord glory and strength!
Ascribe to the Lord glory due his name ...
Say among the nations, "The Lord reigns!" (Ps 96:3a, 7-8a, 10a)

The Lord reigns ...
Clouds and thick darkness are round about him;

righteousness and justice are the foundation of his throne ...
The heavens proclaim his righteousness;
and the peoples behold his glory. (Ps 97:1-2, 6)

Ascribe to the Lord, O heavenly beings,
ascribe to the Lord glory and strength.
Ascribe to the Lord the glory of his name;
worship the Lord in holy array.
The voice of the Lord is upon the waters;
the God of glory thunders,
the Lord, upon many waters ...
The voice of the Lord makes the oaks to whirl,
and strips the forests bare;
and in his temple all cry, "Glory!"
The Lord sits enthroned over the flood;
the Lord sits enthroned as king for ever. (Ps 29:1-3, 9-10)

Lift up your heads, O Gates!
and be lifted, O ancient doors!
that the King of glory may come in.
Who is the king of glory?
The Lord, strong and mighty,
the Lord, mighty in battle!
Lift up your heads, O gates!
and be lifted up, O ancient doors!
that the King of glory may come in.
Who is this King of glory?
The Lord of hosts,
he is the King of glory! (Ps 24:7-10)

I will extol thee, my God and my King,
and bless thy name for ever and ever ...
On the glorious splendor (*kebod* [*kabod*] *hodeka*) of thy majesty,
and on thy wondrous works, I will meditate ...
They shall speak of the glory of thy kingdom,
and tell of thy power,
to make known to the sons of men thy mighty deeds,
and the glorious splendor (*kebod* [*kabod*] *hodeka*) of thy kingdom.
(Ps 145:1, 5, 12)

Let Israel be glad in his Maker,
let the sons of Zion rejoice in their King! ...

> Let the faithful exult in glory;
>> let them sing for joy on their couches. (Ps 149:2, 5)

In the year that King Uzziah died I saw the Lord sitting upon a throne, high and lifted up; and his train filled the temple...And one [of the seraphim] called to another and said: "Holy, holy, holy is the Lord of hosts; the whole earth is full of his glory."... And I said: "Woe is me! For I am lost...for my eyes have seen the King, the Lord of hosts!" (Is 6:1, 3, 5)

These are only the most obvious examples of the link between "glory" and God's kingship. A close look at other occurrences of *kabod* will show that they provide the same kind of evidence, though less direct. They allude to the theme of God's kingship by mentioning: (a) the heavens, the temple/sanctuary, or Zion, where God resides seated on his throne; or (b) other gods, kings, or nations; or (c) psalmody (or praise) in honor of God.[12]

> The heavens are telling the glory of God;
>> and the firmament proclaims his handiwork. (Ps 19:1)

> O Lord, I love the habitation of thy house,
>> and the place where thy glory dwells. (Ps 26:8)

> So I have looked upon thee in the sanctuary,
>> beholding thy power and glory. (Ps 63:2)

> Make a joyful noise to God, all the earth;
>> sing the glory of his name;
>> give to him glorious praise! (Ps 66:1-2)

> Pour out thy anger on the nations
>> that do not know thee,
>> and on the kingdoms
>> that do not call on thy name! ...
> Help us, O God of our salvation,
>> for the glory of thy name ...
> Why should the nations say,
>> "Where is their God?" (Ps 79:6, 9a, 10a; see also Ps 115:1-2)

> I would rather be a doorkeeper in the house of my God
>> than dwell in the tents of wickedness.
> For the Lord God is a sun and shield;
>> he bestows favor and honor (*kabod*). (Ps 84:10b-11a)

12. On the first two groups see ch.2; on the last, see, e.g., Ps 47, 95, 96, 98, 99, 100.

The nations will fear the name of the Lord,
   and all the kings of the earth thy glory.
For the Lord will build up Zion,
   he will appear in his glory. (Ps 102:15-16)

Praise the Lord!
   Praise, O servants of the Lord,
   praise the name of the Lord!..
The Lord is high above the nations,
   and his glory above the heavens!
Who is like the Lord our God,
   who is seated on high
   who looks far down
upon the heavens and the earth? (Ps 113:1, 4-6)

All the kings of the earth shall praise thee, O Lord,
   for they have heard the words of thy mouth;
   and they shall sing of the ways of the Lord,
   for great is the glory of the Lord. (Ps 138:4-5)

God's Name

References to the *šem* (name) of God almost without exception occur in texts that also refer to his kingship. These texts either identify him directly as king[13] or discuss matters related to his kingship, such as creation,[14] the divine throne,[15] the sanctuary,[16] victory/salvation,[17] the word *sur* (rock, mountain, fortress),[18] and glory.[19] In the ancient Near East, a person's or an object's name was held to encompass the very essence of the named object or

13. Ps 5:2 and 11; 44:4-5; 74:10 and 12; 89:16-18; 99:4 and 6; 145:1-2; 149:2-3.
14. Ps 33:6-7 and 21; 75:1-3; 89:11-12; 124:8; 148:3-6.
15. Ps 9:2, 4-7, 10; 33:14, 21; 75:1-2; 80:1, 18; 86:9, 12; 99:1-6; 113:1, 5.
16. Ps 20:1-2; 52:8-9; 61:4-5; 63:2-4; 69:35-36; 74:7; 76:1-2; 102:15-16; 118:26-27; 122:1-4; 129:5, 8; 135:1-3; 138:2; 149:2-3.
17. Ps 8:1-2; 9:2-3; 18:49-50; 20:5-7; 22:22-24; 44:7-8; 48:10; 54; 66:1-4; 68:1-4; 69:29-30; 74:10-11, 18, 21-22; 79:6, 9; 83:13-18; 89:24-25; 91:14-16; 92:1 and 9-11; 96:2; 103:1, 6; 106:8, 47; 109:20-29; 111:9; 116:4, 13, 17; 118:10-12; 135:13-14; 140:9-13; 142:6b-7a; 143:11-12.
18. Ps 31:3-4; 61:3 and 6; 89:24 and 26; 92:1 and 15.
19. Ps 8:1-2 and 9; 29:1-2; 63:2-4; 66:1-4; 79:9; 86:11-12; 89:16-17; 96:7-8; 99:5-6; 100:4; 102:15-16; 105:1-3; 106:47; 111:9; 113:1-4; 115:1; 148:13.

person;[20] hence the equivalence between God and his name in expressions like "calling upon the name of God"[21] and "praising/blessing the name of God".[22] In the case of a person, his "essence" in this sense would also include all of his possessions that allow him to survive, and thus to "be"[23] as well as his progeny,[24] by which his existence is perpetuated. So if someone's name is "cut off,"[25] "erased/blotted out,"[26] or "destroyed,"[27] or if it "perishes,"[28] then not only has the person perished, but so also have all of his progeny and belongings, with neither a material nor a spiritual legacy living on after him. Conversely, a name is said to be perpetuated, or "raised,"[29] when someone's progeny is secured (Deut 25:5-7).

One way a name can be perpetuated is through remembrance of it: "Now Absalom in his lifetime had taken and set up for himself the pillar which is in the King's valley, for he said, '*I have no son to keep my name in remembrance*'; he called the pillar after his own name, and it is called Absalom's monument to this day." (2 Sam 18:18) "Monument" here renders the Hebrew *yad* (hand). The connection between hand and name can be clearly seen in the following oracle of the Lord:

> To the eunuchs who keep my sabbaths,
>   who choose the things that please me
>   and hold fast my covenant,
>   I will give in my house and within my walls
>   a monument (*yad*) and a name
>   better than sons and daughters;

20. See vol.1, p.46.
21. Ps 80:18-19; 99:6; 105:1; 116:2 and 4, 13, 17.
22. Ps 18:49; 22:22; 66:4; 68:4; 69:30; 86:9, 12; 92:1; 96:1-2; 100:4; 113:1-3; 135:1-3; 145:1-2; 148:1-5; 13-14; 149:1-3.
23. See Num 27:1-4.
24. See Gen 48:15-16; Ps 45:16-17; Is 66:22.
25. *karat*, Josh 7:9; Ruth 4:10; Is 14:22-23; Zeph 1:4.
26. *mahah*, Deut 9:14; 2 Kg 14:27.
27. *nišmad*, 1 Sam 24:21; Is 48:19.
28. *'abad*, Deut 7:24; 12:3; Ps 41:5.
29. The Hebrew verb is *heqim* from *qum* (to stand, rise).

> I will give them an everlasting name
> which shall not be cut off. (Is 56:4-5)

Thus, remembrance is recollection of someone's actions, since this is the connotation entailed in the term *yad* in this context. The words "name" and "fame,"[30] are also related in this way, as are "name" and "glory."[31] In the case of God, who has no progeny, remembrance of his name is equivalent to remembering his "deeds" of creation as well as of victory/salvation; and in fact a parallel between *yad* on the one hand, and power,[32] (mighty) acts,[33] works,[34] or deeds,[35] on the other hand, is a commonplace in the book of Psalms.

---

30. 1 Sam 18:30; 2 Sam 23:18, 22; 1 Kg 4;31; Ps 72:17; Jer 48:17; Ezek 16:15; 39:13.
31. See above.
32. Ps 17:13-14a; 31:8, 15; 37:33; 49:16; 63:10 (the power [*yad*] of the sword); 89:48; etc.
33. Ps 44:2.
34. Ps 8:6a; 19:1; 22:20; 28:4-5; etc.
35. Ps 26:10; 39:10; 58:2; etc.

5

The Relationship Between Heavenly King and Earthly King

Suzerain and Vassal

It is clear from a number of passages that the monarch's kingship is granted to him by God and thus that he is in effect a vassal king under God's suzerainty:

Why do the nations conspire,
and the peoples plot in vain?
The kings of the earth set themselves,
and the rulers take counsel together,
against the Lord and his anointed, saying,
"Let us burst their bonds asunder,
and cast their cords from us."
He who sits in the heavens laughs;
the Lord has them in derision.
Then he will speak to them in his wrath,
and terrify them in his fury, saying,
"I have set my king
on Zion, my holy hill." (Ps 2:1-6)[1]

My heart overflows with a goodly theme;
I address my verses to the king;
my tongue is like the pen of a ready scribe.
You are the fairest of the sons of men;
grace is poured upon your lips;
therefore God has blessed you for ever ...
Your divine throne endures for ever and ever ...
Therefore God, your God, has anointed you
with the oil of gladness above your fellows. (Ps 45:1-2, 6a, 7bc)

1. See also Ps 21:3; 89:3-4, 19-21, 35-37; 132:10-12, 17-18.

The Lord says to my lord:
   "Sit at my right hand,
   till I make your enemies
   your footstool." (Ps 110:1)

Give the king thy justice, O God,
   and thy righteousness to the royal son!
May he judge thy people with righteousness,
   and thy poor with justice! (Ps 72:1-2)

In general, the psalms commonly considered to be "royal" (2, 18, 20, 21, 45, 72, 89, 101, 110, 132, and 144)[2] describe the monarch with terminology used elsewhere to describe the deity, but they present the monarch as a subject of the divine king. Except for Ps 101, all of them say God enthrones the king, and all of them deal with God's kingship either exclusively (Ps 20, 21, 144) or in conjunction with the monarch's. As for Ps 101, it is strictly a king's prayer expressing his intent to do justice; it is a plea of innocence by a "subject" to his "lord."

The king's subservience to God can be gathered from a series of striking features found in the royal psalms. He addresses God as *'eli* (my God, 18:2, 21; 89:26), *'elohay* (my God, 18:6, 21, 29), *'elohe yiš'i* (the God of my salvation, 18:46), *qeren yiš'i* (the horn of my salvation, 18:2), *suri* (my Rock/Mountain/Fortress, 18:2, 46; 144:1), *sur yešu'ati* (the Rock/Mountain/Fortress of my salvation, 89:26). The king is primarily God's *'ebed* (servant, 89:3, 20, 39, 50; 132:10; 144:10) and calls him *'adonay* (my lord, 89:50, 51).[3] He himself is not a god but a *geber* (young, strong man),[4] *'adam* or *'enoš* (man, human being), *ben 'adam* or *ben 'enoš* (man, human being; literally, "son of man"). Ps 89 presents a clear example of this relationship. The king himself is praying in this text, and after complaining that the Lord has put him to shame, he adds:

2. A psalm is referred to as "royal" by scholars when the king is considered to be its subject matter; see more on this below.

3. See also 2:4 and 110:5 where God is addressed as *'adonay* in conjunction with a reference to the king.

4. Similar to *gibbor* which means mighty/strong/elite warrior.

How long, O Lord? Wilt thou hide thyself for ever?
How long will thy wrath burn like fire?
Remember, O Lord, what the measure of life is,
for what vanity thou hast created all the sons of men (*bene 'adam*)!
What man (*geber*) can live and never see death?
Who can deliver his soul from the power of Sheol?
Lord, where is thy steadfast love of old,
which by thy faithfulness thou didst swear to David?[5]
Remember, O Lord, how *thy servant* is scorned;
how I bear in my bosom the insults of the peoples,
with which thy enemies taunt, O Lord,
with which they mock the footsteps of thy anointed. (vv.46-51)

A similar instance is found in the royal psalm 144:

Blessed be the Lord, my rock,
who trains my hands for war, and my fingers for battle;
my rock and my fortress,
my stronghold and my deliverer, my shield and he in whom I take refuge,
who subdues the peoples under him.[6]
O Lord, what is man (*'adam*) that thou dost regard him,
or the son of man (*ben 'enoš*) that thou dost think of him?
Man (*'adam*) is like a breath,
his days are like a passing shadow ...
Stretch forth thy hand from on high,
rescue me and deliver me from the many waters,
from the hands of aliens. (vv.1-4, 7)

It is only when and because someone, a "son of man," is "chosen" (89:3, 19) and "anointed" (2:2; 45:7; 18:50; 20:6; 89:38, 51; 132:10, 17) by God that he becomes God's "son" (2:7; 89:27; 2 Sam 7:14) and acquires the (divine) attributes of his "father" (89:26), i.e., that he becomes "king" (20:9; 21:1, 7; 45:1, 5; 72:1) and *'adon* (master, lord; 45:11; 110:1). Still, even then he remains God's "king" (2:6; 18:50)[7] and thus God's vassal.

The king's vassalage to God can also be seen in that his battle

5. See vv.3-4, 19-20, 28-33.
6. Many manuscripts read "me" instead of "him."
7. See also 21:3a; 89:19b; 110:1; 132:11.

is essentially God's. It is God who prepares (Ps 18:32, 39) and trains (18:33-34; 144:1) the king for combat; God even does the actual fighting for his vassal (Ps 18:16-19, 40-41; 21:8-12; 89:23; 132:18a; 144:7, 10-11). The king's enemies are none other than God's.[8] The external enemies are called waves/breakers (2 Sam 22:5a), torrents (Ps 18:4b//2 Sam 22:5b), waters (Ps 18:16), sea (Ps 89:25a), and river (Ps 89:25b), i.e., names similar to what we saw in Ps 93; whereas the enemies within are *reša'* (wickedness, Ps 45:7) and the *reša'im* (the wicked ones, Ps 101:8), as well as *ra'* (evil, Ps 101:4).

These enemies are overcome not by the king's own power but by God's power, as the use of the word *yamin* (right hand) demonstrates.[9] The exaltation of God's *yamin* (Ps 89:13) is an essential feature of his kingly rule (vv.5-18), while the monarch's *yamin* must be upheld by God over the raging waters (v.25) in order for his kingship to be secure (vv.19-37)—and God could just as easily cause that kingship to be shaken (vv.38-45) by exalting instead the king's foes' *yamin* (v.42).[10] It is the divine *yamin* that battles on behalf of the king (Ps 20:6; 21:8); indeed, the king is seated at God's *yamin* (Ps 110:1). It is the power of God's *yamin* that gives to the king's *yamin* the power to do the *nora'ot* (awesome deeds, Ps 45:4)[11] of the awesome (*nora'*) God (Ps 89:8).[12]

Since the king attains victory over his enemies thanks to divine help, his victory brings glory and fame to God's name (Ps 89:17; Ps 18:50; 20:1, 5, 7; 89:17, 24) as well as his own (Ps 21:5; 45:17; 72:17). Consequently, the king must always celebrate his victories by means of offerings and sacrifices to his deity (Ps 96:8; 20:3), and those victories are depicted as having actually been imple-

8. Ps 2:1-3; 20:6-8, 9; 18:3 and 6, 16-19; 21:8-12; 89:10 and 42, 51; 132:18.

9. The Hebrew term *yamin* (right [hand]) reflects the idea of power inherent in the *yad* (hand) with which one acts. See above.

10. See also Ps 144:8, 11.

11. See also Ps 65:6; 106:22; 145:5.

12. See also Ps 47:2; 66:3; 68:35; 76:7, 12; 96:4; 99:3; 111:9.

mented from the heavenly abode: (a) the Lord is called a "rock" (*sela'*),[13] fortress,[14] rock/mountain (*sur*),[15] stronghold;[16] (b) he rides on a cherub,[17] bows down the heavens, and comes down from on high;[18] (c) he is seated in his heavenly sanctuary[19] from which he sends help.[20]

The king is victorious not only because of God's help but also because God delegates his own divine prerogatives and duties to his vassal the king. Like God, the king has dominion over his realm:

> May he [the king] have dominion from sea to sea,
>   and from the River to the ends of the earth!
> May his foes bow down before him,
>   and his enemies lick the dust!
> May the kings of Tarshish and of the isles render him tribute,
>   may the kings of Sheba and Seba bring gifts!
> May all kings fall down before him,
>   all nations serve him! (Ps 72:8-11)[21]

The king's appointed role as enthroned ruler is so important that it typically overshadows his person. Indeed, there is nothing personal, by our standards, about the king. Even for his wedding he is depicted in general terms as king rather than as a specific individual: the part of the nuptial psalm 45 dedicated to the groom is mainly a description of his kingly attributes of victory and justice (vv.3-7a). Even his own bride is portrayed as one of his subdued subjects. Addressing her, the psalmist says: "Since he [the king] is your lord, bow to him" (v.11b)! And things cannot be otherwise since, once they are wedded, "they enter the palace *of the king*" (v.15b) and the king is *enthroned* there.

13. Ps 18:2.
14. Ps 18:2; 144:1.
15. Ps 18:2, 31; 144:1.
16. Ps 18:2; 144:1.
17. Ps 18:10.
18. Ps 18:9, 16; 144:5, 7; also 20:6b.
19. Ps 89:5-14; also 132:8-9.
20. Ps 20:2.
21. See also Ps 18:47.

Divine Justice Executed by the King

One of the key duties delegated by God to the king is the administration of justice. Since, after all, the poor and needy the king is supposed to care for (Ps 72:12-14) belong to God (v.2), kingly righteousness (vv.2, 3) must be based upon divine righteousness (v.1). Actually, in Ps 72 the king's dominion (vv.8-12) and prosperity under his rule (vv.5-7, 15-17) are conditional upon his righteousness (vv.1-4 and 12-14). This is such an important conception that the royal psalm 101 is entirely dedicated to that aspect of the kingly rule:

> I will sing of loyalty (*hesed*) and justice (*mišpat*);
>> to thee, O Lord, I will sing.
> I will give heed to the way (*derek*) that is blameless (*tamim*).
> Oh when wilt thou come to me?
> I will walk with integrity (*tam*) of heart within my house.
> I will not set before my eyes anything that is base.
> I hate the work of those who fall away;
>> it shall not cleave to me.
> Perverseness of heart shall be far from me;
> I will know nothing of evil (*ra'*).
> Him who slanders his neighbor secretly
> I will destroy.
> The man of haughty looks and arrogant heart
> I will not endure.
> I will look with favor on the faithful of the land,
>> that they may dwell with me;
> he who walks in the way that is blameless (*tamim*)
> shall minister to me.
> No man who practices deceit
> shall dwell in my house;
> no man who utters lies
> shall continue in my presence
> Morning by morning I will destroy
> all the wicked in the land,
>> cutting off all the evildoers
> from the city of the Lord.

Hence, like God, the king is also both the *saddiq* (righteous one,

Ps 72:7a)[22] and the *hasid* (the one who shows *hesed*,[23] Ps 18:25a; 89:15a) par excellence. He is the consummate *tamim* (blameless one, Ps 18:24, 25b) as well; like God who "shows himself blameless" (*tittammad*, *tam*) and whose way is perfect (*tamim*; Ps 18:25, 30), he "walks with integrity (*tam*) of heart" and his "household/palace (*bayit*)" consists of people who also "walk in the way (*derek*) that is blameless (*tamim*)" (Ps 101:2b, 6-7a).

The king is to be *tamim* as God is by "walking in God's way," i.e., by obeying God's law (*torah*) and its *mišpatim* (ordinances/judgments), *huqqot* (statutes), and *miswot* (commandments):

> The Lord rewarded me according to my righteousness;
>> according to the cleanness of my hands he recompensed me.
> For I have kept the ways of the Lord,
> and have not wickedly departed from my God.
> For all his ordinances (*mišpatayw, mišpatim*) were before me,
> and his statutes (*huqqotayw, huqqot*) I did not put away from me.
> I was blameless (*tamim*) before him,
> and I kept myself from guilt.
> Therefore the Lord has recompensed me according to my righteousness;
> according to the cleanness of my hands in his sight. (Ps 18:20-24)

> If his [David's] children forsake my law (*torati, torah*)
> and do not walk according to my ordinances (*mišpatay, mišpatim*),
> if they violate my statutes (*huqqotay, huqqot*)
> and do not keep my commandments (*miswotay, miswot*),
> then I will punish their transgression (*piš'am, peša'*) with the rod,[24]
> and their iniquity with scourges. (Ps 89:30-32)

A comparison between these last two passages and Ps 101 will

22. The immediate context (vv.5-7) as well as the broader one (vv.2-4, 8-12, and 15-17) form a prayer on behalf of the king. Thus, Dahood's interpretation of *saddiq* as "the just man" in a general sense (II, p.181) is unwarranted. The RSV follows the few manuscripts that read *sedeq* (righteousness) and that are followed by the Septuagint and the Syriac versions; their emendation is based on the belief that v.7 refers to the king as do vv.5-6. Thus the accurate translation of v.7a is: "May the righteous one, i.e., the king, flourish in/during his days ..." Calling the king *saddiq* perfectly fits the intent of Ps 72.

23. See ch.4.

24. See Is 11:4.

readily show that the king is bound to rule his own "house" (palace) and city the same way the Lord rules His "house" (sanctuary) and city, i.e., according to the divine *torah* (law). The obvious reason is that the royal city is ultimately the Lord's city. A famous example expressing this reality is the stele, now at the Louvre Museum in Paris, on which is inscribed the code of laws of Hammurabi, the sixth king of the First Dynasty of Babylon (early second millennium B.C.). At the top of the stele there is a bas-relief showing the sun-deity Shamash, god of justice, commissioning King Hammurabi to write down the laws of the city of Babylon. Deuteronomy presents us with a similar view of kingship and law:

> And when he [the king] sits on the throne of his kingdom, he shall write for himself in a book a copy of this law (*torah*), from that which is in the charge of the Levitical priests; and it shall be with him, and he shall read in it all the days of his life, that he may learn to fear the Lord his God, by keeping all the words of this law (*torah*) and these statutes (*huqqim*),[25] and doing them; *that his heart may not be lifted up above his brethren,* and that he may not turn aside from the commandment (*miswah*),[26] either to the right hand or to the left; *so that he may continue long in his kingdom, he and his children,*[27] in Israel. (17:18-20)

Thus, divinity, kingship, and the city commonwealth, i.e., the people or citizenry, were materially bound together through the law that was *concurrently* a divine, royal, and social reality. Yet, since the (divine) law was de facto promulgated by the king, and thus originated from him, it was through *his* implementation of the law and *his* example of abiding by it fully, that the people, as *his* subjects, shared in the divine victory granted to *him*. Notice the alternation between "you/he" referring to the king and "we" referring to the people in Ps 20:

> The Lord answer you in the day of trouble!
>   The name of the God of Jacob protect you!

25. Similar to *huqqot*.
26. The singular form of *miswot*.
27. See Ps 45:16; 132:11-12.

May he send you help from the sanctuary,
and give you support from Zion!
May he remember all your offerings,
and regard with favor your burnt sacrifices!
May he grant you your heart's desire,
and fulfill all your plans!
May we shout for joy over your victory,
and in the name of our God set up our banners!
May the Lord fulfill all your petitions!
Now I[28] know that the Lord will help his anointed;
he will answer him from his holy heaven
with mighty victories by his right hand.
Some boast of chariots, and some of horses;
but we boast of the name of the Lord our God.
They will collapse and fall;
but we shall rise and stand upright.
Give victory to the king, O Lord;
answer us when we call.[29]

In Ps 89, the king beseeches God to overlook his sin of failing to uphold the law (vv.30-32), to remember His promise to David (vv.3-4, 19-29, 33-37), and to turn the odds (vv.46-51) by granting the king victory over the enemies God had unleashed against him (vv.38-45). Yet, in the middle of his prayer he exclaims:

Blessed are *the people* who know the festal shout,
who walk, O Lord, in the light of thy countenance,
who exult in your name all the day,
and extol thy righteousness.
For thou art the glory of *their* strength;
by thy favor *our* horn is exalted.
For *our* shield belongs to the Lord,
our king to the Holy one of Israel.[30]   (vv.15-18)

---

28. I.e., the psalmist, either priest or cultic prophet.
29. See also "Be exalted, O Lord, in thy strength! We will sing and praise thy power" at the end of Ps 21.
30. Dahood's translation of v.18 makes more sense: "Truly Yahweh is our Suzerain, the Holy One of Israel our King!" (II, p.309)

6

The King's Prayers

The King As High Priest

The uniqueness of the king as the medium between deity and people makes out of him the point of contact between them in either direction. He not only acts on behalf of the deity toward the people but also intercedes with the deity on behalf of his subjects. This explains why, at the inauguration of the Jerusalem temple, Solomon prays both for himself and his people. He begins by praying to God on behalf of himself as king; the prayer is clearly by and for one individual, and the repeated references to David and his sons indicate that this individual's status as king is the theme of the prayer:

> [O Lord] who has kept with thy servant David my father what thou didst declare to him; yea, thou didst speak with thy mouth, and with thy hand hast fulfilled it this day. Now therefore, O Lord, God of Israel, keep with thy servant David my father what thou hast promised him, saying, "There shall never fail you a man before me to sit upon the throne of Israel, if only your sons take heed to their way, to walk before me as you have walked before me." Now therefore, O God of Israel, let thy word be confirmed, which thou hast spoken to thy servant David my father...Yet have regard to the prayer of thy servant and to his supplication, O Lord my God, hearkening to the cry and to the prayer which thy servant prays before thee this day; that thy eyes may be open night and day toward this house, the place of which thou hast said, "My name shall be there," that thou mayest hearken to the prayer which thy servant offers toward this place. (1 Kg 8:24-26, 28-29)

Then, again *as king*, he proceeds to present a petition for his people, whom he refers to as "thy servants" (vv.32, 36), as a (high) priest would:

And hearken thou to the supplication of thy servant and of thy people Israel, when they pray toward this place; yea, hear thou in heaven thy dwelling place; and when thou hearest, forgive...then hear thou in heaven their prayer and their supplication...Let thy eyes be open to the supplication of thy servant, and to the supplication of thy people Israel, giving ear to them whenever they call to thee...(vv.30, 45, 52)

He also blesses the people (v.55), offers sacrifices (vv.62-64), and personally consecrates the temple (vv.63b-64a).

The parallelism between deity and king is complete. And the correspondence applies not only to the throne but also extends to the sanctuary. This is reflected in the fact that the words *hekal* (temple or palace) and *bayit* (house) are used interchangeably to mean either the sanctuary—be it heavenly or earthly—or the royal residence. God's vassal is also his priest, exactly as a tribal patriarch would be. Put otherwise, *the* supplicant par excellence is none other than the king; he is *the* servant of God, and his subjects are God's servants only indirectly. Consequently, no prayer can be raised in the temple unless he himself is uttering it; the sanctuary is, after all, *his.* The main reason why the people rejected the preaching of Amos and Jeremiah lay precisely in the fact that these prophets did not reflect the official point of view, the standpoint of the "crown" or the "presidency," as we would put it today. The critical words of the prophets were perceived as treason worthy of the death sentence!

Then Amaziah the priest of Bethel sent to Jeroboam king of Israel, saying, "Amos has conspired against you in the midst of the house of Israel; the land is not able to hear his words..." And Amaziah said to Amos, "...never again prophesy at Bethel, for it is the king's sanctuary, and it is a temple of the kingdom." (Am 7:10, 13)

The priests and the prophets and all the people heard Jeremiah speaking these words in the house of the Lord. And when Jeremiah finished speaking all that the Lord had commanded him to speak to all the people, then the priests and the prophets and all the people laid hold of him, saying, "You shall die! Why have you prophesied in the name of the Lord, saying, 'This house shall be like Shiloh, and this city shall be desolate, without inhabitant'"? (Jer 26:7-9)

The King As the Subject of the "Individual" Prayer

One may not, then, imagine—though many contemporary scholars still do—that some of the psalms are "individual" prayers. Since the most common situation of distress encountered in the so-called "laments of the individual"[1] is sickness, some scholars point to Hezekiah's recitation of a psalm on his sickbed (2 Kg 20:1-11//Is 38:1-8) as evidence that the psalm is "individual" in nature. Besides the fact that this is the only such instance in the entire Old Testament—outside the book of Psalms—where a sick person recites a psalm, what they fail to notice is that the king is no mere "individual," and his death would be more a *national* calamity than a personal one.[2] This is made clear within the texts that recount this episode:

1) Isaiah is commissioned to inform the king of God's acceptance of his petition in the following terms: "Turn back, and say to Hezekiah the prince of my people, Thus says the Lord, *the God of David your father*: I have heard your prayer, I have seen your tears; behold, I will heal you; on the third day you shall go up to the house of the Lord. And I will add fifteen years to your life. *I will deliver you and this city* out of the hand of the king of Assyria, *and defend this city* for my own sake and *for my servant David's sake*." (2 Kg 20:5-6). This is God's response to someone who had not even mentioned anything about Jerusalem in his prayer! (2 Kg 20:3//Is 38:3)[3]

2) Hezekiah "turned his face to the wall, and prayed to the Lord" in 2 Kg 20:2. What wall? Consider 2 Chr 29:6, which presents a speech of Hezekiah delivered when he "opened the doors of the house of the Lord": "For our fathers have been

1. Psalms that express a complaint to the deity by an individual experiencing hardship.
2. See chs.1 and 5.
3. And what he did pray was a kingly prayer: "Remember now, O Lord, I beseech thee, how I have walked before thee in faithfulness (*'emet*) and with a whole heart, and have done what is good in thy sight." The word *'emet* here is decisive in identifying this as a kingly prayer (see above regarding the royal qualities of *hesed* and *'emet*.

unfaithful and have done what was evil in the sight of the lord our
God; they have forsaken him, and have *turned away their faces*[4]
from the habitation of the Lord, and turned their backs." Given
this emphasis on turning toward the temple, turning *toward* "the
wall" in 2 Kg 20:2 must have implied turning toward the temple
itself; perhaps the wall was adjacent to the temple or on the side of
the palace nearest the temple. Otherwise, why would the king not
simply "turn his face" to the Lord? The importance of the temple
may also be seen in God's command that Hezekiah go up to the
sanctuary after his healing (2 Kg 20:5). Isaiah tells us that while
there he prayed a psalm *as though he were sick* (Is 38:10-20). In
other words, prayer is essentially done at the temple, which is
essentially the king's (personal) sanctuary.[5]

The other instance sometimes cited in support of the theory of
"individual psalms" is the case of Hannah, Samuel's mother, in 1
Sam 1-2. But it too shows instead the royal nature of the psalms.
It is at Shiloh, where Hannah yearly "went up to the house of the
Lord," (1:7) where she "prayed before the Lord," (1:12) and
where she later comes for her thanksgiving prayer: "Oh, my lord
[the priest Eli]! As you live, my lord, I am the woman who was
standing here in your presence, praying before the Lord." (1:26)
Furthermore, the psalm she proceeds to pray ends by speaking of
the king: "The Lord will judge the ends of the earth; he will give
strength to his king, and exalt the power of his anointed." (2:10b)
That is, she prays a *kingly* psalm! The conclusion is unavoidable:
not only does one pray at the deity's shrine which at the same time
is the king's sanctuary, but one also prays with the king's own
words! One may not retroject into the ancient Near East our
contemporary setting where prayer can be formulated ad hoc by
any individual to the "universal" and "ubiquitous" God[6] at any
moment and any place of one's choosing.

4. The same verb used in 2 Kg 20:2//Is 38:2.

5. Am 7:10-11. See also vol.1, p.12 and vol.2, p.75.

6. See chs.2 and 3.

Most Psalms are Royal

Also insupportable is the assertion that other psalms originated in "family" circles, as though the ancient Near East was a kind of a Europe or North America between the 17th and 20th centuries, where the family head would recite an ad hoc "psalm" at the dinner table, or around the bed of a sick family member, or at the occasion of any given calamity or joyful event. Some want us even to believe that "lament psalms" were used at times of crisis in the circle of family and caring friends, under the direction of a ritual expert! These groups are even likened to contemporary group therapy under the direction of an expert in such processes![7] I will not argue against the fact that the ancient Near East used official "wailers" to express outwardly the feeling of sorrow and thus help relieve the psychological pressure of the stricken. However, wailing was used at the occasion of an *irreversible* catastrophe, whether personal, such as death,[8] or collective, such as the destruction of a city[9] or the total defeat of a nation.[10] Moreover, the fact that dirges or laments followed a pattern, both materially and formally, known in Hebrew poetry as *qinah*,[11] clearly indicates they generally were not ad hoc compositions but rather traditional poems that fitted specific occasions. Nothing seems to have essentially changed since those times. Our contemporary version of this "general" or "traditional" approach to momentous occasions in life are found in the following examples: gift shop cards for different occasions; wedding toasts or songs; traditional texts one chooses from at funeral homes; etc. In all these instances the "personal" touch is simply an "added" feature and occurs primarily on the level of the name of the addressee.

7. See e.g. E. S. Gerstenberger, *Psalms: Part I with an Introduction to Cultic Poetry*, Grand Rapids, 1988, referred to by James Limburg, "Psalms, Book of," in David Noel Freedman, ed., *The Anchor Bible Dictionary*, vol.5, p.525.

8. Gen 50:10; 2 Sam 1:17; 2 Chr 35:24-25; Jer 31:15.

9. Jer 9:10-11, 20-21; Ezek 2:10 and 4:1-3; 19; 26:17; 27:2, 32; 28:12; Am 5:16-17.

10. Jer 6:26; 7:28-29; 9:10-11; 48:38; Lam 2:5; Ezek 19; 26:17; 27:2, 32; 32:2, 16; Am 5:1-2; 8:7-8; Mic 2:4.

11. See my comments on Am 5:1 in vol.2, p.53.

The point here is that even though a family might make use of a psalm or a prayer, that text will have originated elsewhere. I am not suggesting that prayer originated in the city setting; it was definitely known already at the tribal level. But since it was addressed to the deity, it was usually conducted at the deity's shrine, and by the deity's official channel, either the patriarch or the priest assigned to a particular shrine. Put otherwise, prayer was essentially an official, not personal, matter. And this is logical in a society where the deity was tribal, not personal.[12] The same held true in kingly societies where the deity was associated with a city or nation, or with a king.[13] Here too, things have basically remained unchanged over the centuries. Take the following examples:

1) In the Middle Ages, in both Eastern and Western Europe, nations were baptized after the manner of their leader. *First* he endorsed the Christian faith, *then* his subjects followed suit. We have the examples of Khan Boris and the Bulgarians in 864, and Prince Vladimir and the Rus' in 989.

2) During the Reformation movement in the Western church in the 16th century, oddly enough an issue that started as an uncompromising stand for the "gospel" and "personal faith," found its practical solution in Germany, Luther's home ground, on the basis of the principle of *cujus regio hujus religio* (whoever rules the principality chooses the religion of that principality). To avoid continuous bloodshed, it was decided that every prince would choose his personal allegiance, either to Roman Catholicism or to Protestantism, and his principality would follow suit. Those of his subjects that were dissatisfied would have to relocate to a different principality.

3) Even now in Western Europe, the monarch of the Netherlands is to be of the Reformed faith, while the British monarch is ex officio member and head of the Anglican church.

12. See ch.1.
13. See ch.5.

All this means that at the sanctuary, which was both divine and kingly, the praying entity was either the monarch or the nation, but never the individual subject. Prayer was ultimately uttered either by or in behalf of the king.[14] Consequently, the prayer of an "individual in distress"—whether uttered by him or by a priest on his behalf—was either a kingly psalm or patterned after one, as the terminology used in most psalms will readily show. Which explains the following statement by M. Dahood in the Introduction to his *Psalms III*:

> Scholars generally classify eleven psalms as royal, that is, psalms sung on festive occasions for or in honor of the king and the royal house. These are 2, 18, 20, 21, 45, 72, 89, 101, 110, 132, 144. To this list the following may now be added: 3, 22, 27 (though not yet recognized in *Psalms I*), 41 (possibly), 54, 57, 59, 61, 63, 86, 91, 92, 102, 127, 130, 138, 143.[15]
>
> Some of the verbal clues that help identify these psalms as royal are: *šem*, "name"; *'anah*, "to conquer"; *'ebed*, "servant", *hesed we'emet*, kindness and fidelity"; *'adonay*, "my Lord; *kabod*, "glory"; *magan*, "Suzerain" (divine title); *suri*, "My Mountain"; *nagid*, "Leader" (divine title); the composite divine name *yhwh 'elyon*, "Yahweh Most High"; the parallelism of *sarah*, "my adversaries," and *'oyebay*, "my foes"; *yamin*, "right hand." In several of these psalms (22:28; 86:9; 102:16, 23; 138:4) the note of universalism coheres with the phrasal evidence to strengthen the royal classification. (p. xxxviii)

A few years later, in his *Kingship and the Psalms*,[16] J. H. Eaton discusses "The growth of royal interpretations" in section 4 of the first chapter entitled "How Many Psalms are Royal? General Arguments." At the end of this section, and immediately after referring to Dahood's three-volume commentary, he writes:

14. E.g. Ps 2; 18; 20; 21; 45; 72; 89, 101; 110; 132; 144. This applies even to the prayers that were presumably taken over from the tribal setting and eventually incorporated into the city temple repertoire.
15. Dahood's original numbering is in Roman numerals; I transcribed the numbers into Arabic numerals to make the text more easily readable. Outside this list Dahood recognizes as royal Ps 28 in his comments on Ps 92, v.16 in *Psalms II*, p. 338.
16. No date, but 1975 at the earliest since the dedication reads as follows: In memory of F. M. LEMOINE O.P. +1975.

Finally here, I venture to refer to my small commentary of 1967. Aware of the many conflicting explanations of the person of 'the psalmist,' of which only a sample has been discussed above, I set out to ponder each psalm with an open mind. Contradictory witnesses such as Kraus and Mowinckel were constantly at my side. The result was that I found a royal interpretation to be the most satisfactory in about the same number of cases as had Mowinckel in *GT*.[17] But what gave me the impetus to write the present book was that in many cases the text seemed to spring to life as a totality only when seen from this point of view. (p.19-20)

Then, on the basis of section 5 of his chapter 1, "General Arguments for extensive royal interpretation," he comes up with the two following lists in chapter 2: (a) Psalms with clearly royal content are 3; 4; 7; 9-10; 17; 22; 23; 27; 28; 35; 40; 41; 57; 59; 61; 62; 63; 66; 69; 70; 71; 75; 89; 91; 92; 94; 108 (together with 44, 60, 74, 80, 83, 84); 118; 138; 140; 143; and (b) Less clear cases are 5; 11; 16; 31; 36; 42-43; 51; 52; 54; 55; 56; 73; 77; 86; 102; 109; 116; 120; 121; 139; 141; 142. In the third section of chapter 2 he enumerates the psalms that "are best not used in the task of reconstructing the royal ideal in the psalms, unless the perspective of scholarship changes considerably": 1; 6; 8; 12; 13; 14; 15; 19; 25; 26; 32; 37; 38; 49; 53; 58; 64; 78; 88; 103; 104; 106; 119; 122; 123; 129; 130; 131; 145; 146. Yet, interestingly enough, he immediately adds: "It is interesting, however, to observe that even in these cases *there is little firm sign of a 'private' psalmody. The style and setting remain preponderantly those of Jerusalem's official cult.*" (p. 86; my italics)

Eaton's last statement puts under serious question Dahood's frequent reference to many psalms as "individual" prayers. However, even Eaton's reluctance to consider certain psalms as royal is unwarranted when one takes into consideration the elements connected with kingship, which I discussed in the previous chapters. In the appendix following this chapter I present some specific

17. Which is his *Det Gamle Testamente* iv.1, Salmeboken, 1955 [my note].

reasons for considering many of the "questionable" psalms to be quite definitely "royal."

Temple Psalmody

Taking into consideration Eaton's comments one can safely add that although the royal character of many other psalms cannot be proven beyond the slightest doubt, their terminology corresponds closely to that of the royal ones, and in any case they do not seem to be "private" in nature. There is no need to go into a detailed discussion of every individual psalm here; what I must stress, however, is that starting with the Davidic-Solomonic period, psalmody in Judah and Israel came strictly under the control of the royal sanctuaries.

Even if one allows the possibility that an oral tradition of psalmody arose outside the realm of the official sanctuaries, one must remember that the book of Psalms was ultimately, together with the rest of the Old Testament, the product of the post-exilic Judahite leadership that was basically priestly and Levitical.[18] Beginning already with the Deuteronomic Reform, which was essentially the work of the Jerusalemite priesthood,[19] virtually all sustained literary activity that eventually became the Old Testament was in the hands of the priestly/Levitical scribes. Not only that, but given the intransigent attitude of the reformers regarding the strict oneness of the Jerusalem temple and its cult, it is hard to imagine that, in their editorial work that produced the Book of (exactly one hundred and fifty canonical) Psalms, they took into consideration anything else besides what was part of the official Jerusalem temple psalmody.

18. See vol.1, pp.135-151.
19. See vol.1, ch.6.

Appendix

Psalm 6

Usually termed an "individual lament for relief from sickness." Yet the mention of *kol soreray* (all my foes, v.7) and the petition that *kol 'oyebay* (all my enemies, v.10) be put to shame militate against a "private" setting, especially if one takes into account the similarity to the case of Hezekiah in Is 38//2 Kg 20.

Psalm 8

A paean of praise to God, beginning and ending with praise of God's name (vv.1a and 9). It is similar to the psalms that exalt God as king and creator in that it: (a) speaks of his glory (v.1b); (b) refers to his creative activity and the world "which thou hast established" (v.3); and (c) mentions his *'oz*—"bulwark" in RSV—against his foes and enemy (v.2). Within this context mention is made of a "man/son of man" whom God "has made little less than *'elohim* (God or the gods)" (v.5a), whom he "crowns with glory and honor (*hadar*)" (v.5b), and "under whose feet he has put all things" (v.6b). Both *hadar* and "under one's feet" occur exclusively in a kingly context. The former is always found in Psalms either in conjunction with God's kingship[20] or creating/redeeming activity,[21] or in reference to the king,[22] while the latter reflects the notion of supremacy[23] or victory.[24]

There is also a striking parallelism between this psalm and the royal psalm 21. Compare "Yet thou...dost *crown* him with *glory* and *honor* (*hadar*)" (Ps 8:5) with "thou dost set a *crown* of fine gold upon his head....His *glory* is great through thy help; splendor and *majesty* (*hadar*) thou dost bestow upon him" (Ps 21:3b, 5). As does Ps 8, Ps 21 mentions God's enemies (v.8) and indirectly calls them "sons of men" (v.10).

Psalm 13

The king expresses his trust in God's *hesed* (steadfast love; v.5a). Notice the first person singular throughout; the title "my God" used to address the Lord (v.3); and the references to the enemy who has been "exalted over me" (v.2b), "rejoices because I am shaken" (v.4b) and says "I have prevailed over him." (v.4a)

Psalm 19

Though the first person singular is not used, we do find a high incidence of other elements found in royal psalms: exaltation of God's creative power (vv.1-6); praise of the divine law (vv.7-10) by which the psalmist is strictly bound (vv.11-13); reference to God as *suri* (my rock, v.14); and reference by the psalmist to himself as "thy [the Lord's] servant" (vv.11 and 13).

20. Ps 29:4; 96:6; 145:5, 12; 149:9.
21. Ps 90:16; 104:1; 111:3.
22. Ps 21:5; 45:3, 4; 110:3.
23. Ps 18:9.
24. Ps 18:38; 110:1.

Psalm 25

Another expression of trust in God in the face of difficulties. Notice the themes of enemies (vv.2 and 19) in connection with shame (vv.2-3);[25] *hesed we'emet* (steadfast love and faithfulness) linked to following God's law (v.10); and the righteous man's progeny who will possess the land (v.13). It also includes a prayer to "the God of my salvation" (v.5) for personal safety associated with a petition for the people's redemption (v.22).

Psalm 37

Here it is the repeated reference to so many "royal" components that ultimately lends to the psalm a "royal" fabric. These components include the *mere'im* (wicked ones/evildoers, vv 1, 9) and *raša'/reša'im* (wicked one[s], vv.10, 12, 14, 16, 17, 20, 21, 32) who wage battle (vv.12, 14-15, 32) and plot (*zamam*, v.12; compare with Ps 31:13b); the *saddiq/saddiqim* (righteous one[s], vv.12, 17, 21, 25, 32); the *tamimim* (blameless ones, 18); the *yišre derek* (those who are upright in their "way"); and *'adonay* (my lord, v.13) who *yishaq* (laughs, v.13; compare with Ps 2:4) at the wicked. The psalmist speaks of the *miš'alot* (desires/petitions, v.4b; compare with Ps 20:5c) of his heart (v.4b; compare with Ps 21:2a); and of "committing his *way* to the Lord" (v.5a;[26] compare with Ps 22:8) by not giving free reign to his own *'ap* (anger, v.8a) and *hemah* (wrath, v.8a), that he might be granted *sedeq* ["vindication" in RSV], v.6a) and *mišpat* ([just] judgment, v.6b) by God. It is in doing so while waiting for the Lord to intervene on his behalf (v.34; compare with Ps 25: 5, 21; 27:14, twice; 39:7a;[27] 40:1; 52:9b[28]), that he and the meek around him will possess the land (vv.11a; 12b; 29) forever through his progeny (vv.27-29).

Psalm 38

A prayer for salvation from a deadly disease by someone who calls upon the deity as *'adonay* (my lord, vv.10, 15) and *'elohay* (my God, vv.15 and 21) and refers to the might and large number of "my foes" (v.19). The enemies' advantage is permitted by God himself (vv.1-2), as in the royal psalm 89 (vv.38-45, especially v.42); that is why the psalmist waits for the Lord to change his mind and fight for, not against, him (vv.15-16; compare with Ps 89:46-51).

Psalm 58

The singular *saddiq* (the righteous one, vv.10 and 11), the imagery of battle (vv.6, 10), the reference to the enemies as "wicked" (vv.3, 10), and the appeal to God to fight on behalf of the psalmist (vv.6-9), when combined, give the psalm a "royal" flavor. Moreover, the opponents are viewed as "gods" or "mighty lords" in a position to judge men, which reflects a setting similar to that of Ps 82 or, at least, a royal one; hence the necessity for divine interference (vv.6-9).

25. Notice also the parallel between v.2 and Ps 22:5 in the reference to "trust in the Lord" and "not being put to shame."

26. Also vv.23b and 31a.

27. Ps 39 is clearly royal: it is a prayer to *'adonay* (my lord, v.7) for salvation from a deadly illness.

28. Translated "I will proclaim" in RSV. Notice the parallel "I trust" in v.8b.

Psalm 64

The enemies are *mere'im* (wicked/evildoers, v.2) who are "plotting" (*sod*, v.2; similar to *nosad* in Ps 2:1 and 31:14b) and waging war (vv.3-4) against the *tam* (blameless one, v.4) and *saddiq* (righteous one, v.10) on whose behalf God himself is battling (vv.7-9). Together with the *saddiq* "all the upright in heart (*yišre leb*) will rejoice" (v.10), i.e., the king and his people.

Psalm 88

As in similar psalms discussed earlier, this "individual" prayer of one stricken with a deadly illness presents a series of "royal" features. The sickness is directly ascribed to God's wrath (*hamah*, v.7a and *haron*, v.16a) without mention of outside enemies. The adversaries are friends that God turned against the psalmist (vv.8, 18). The divine wrath is actually expressed through the mediacy of the *mišbarim* (waves, v.7b) and the *mayim* (waters/flood, v.17). Finally, the psalmist's petition for healing appeals to God's *hesed* (steadfast love, v.11a) and *'emunah* (faithfulness, v.11b).

Prayers for rain

Psalm 4 is part of Eaton's list of "psalms with clearly royal content."[29] A major point in his argumentation is that it is a prayer for the end of a drought, the opposite of which is expressed through the word *tob* (good).[30] Dahood goes a step further and convincingly shows that the Hebrew *tob* in v.6[31] is to be taken as a reference to rain.[32] This clearly fits with the notion I discussed in ch.1 about the king as the source and sustainer of all life in his kingdom. It is reasonable then to consider Ps 65 and 85 as prayers for rain uttered by the king as high priest, on behalf of the people. In its turn, Ps 67 is a public prayer for rain using the "royal" pattern of petition.

---

29. Notice also the psalmist reference to himself as a *hasid* (godly one) to the Lord in v.3.
30. Eaton, pp.29-30.
31. V.7 in Dahood.
32. Dahood I, pp.25-26. See also my comments on Joel 2:23 in ch.4.

7

Exilic and Post-Exilic Psalmody

The natural consequence of the conclusion arrived at in the preceding chapter is that the exilic and post-exilic priestly leadership formulated its official psalmody after the pattern of, and using the phraseology of, the pre-exilic Jerusalem temple. This was an understandable development because the priestly leadership, when praying on behalf of the people, was actually taking the role of the king as high priest. However, due to the anti-monarchical stand of the Deuteronomic Reform[1] that culminated in the priestly vision of a kingless society where the Lord would be the sole ruler of his people without any intermediary,[2] the basic new feature of post-exilic psalmody was the disappearance of the use of the first or third person singular in reference to the king. The post-exilic priestly teaching imbedded in the Pentateuch[3] finds its center in the statement: "For I am the Lord your God; consecrate yourselves therefore, and be holy, for I am holy...For I am the Lord who brought you up out of the land of Egypt, to be your God; you shall therefore be holy, for I am holy." (Lev 11:44-45; also 19:2b; 20:7, 26) This statement is directly addressed to "all the congregation of the people of Israel" (19:2a; also 11:2a; 20:2a), without any reference to the priests as intermediaries for the divine word. In fact, the priests themselves get the message indirectly, since God speaks to Aaron and instructs him to pass on what he hears to the priests (21:1, 6-8).[4] Holiness, which is a strictly divine and thus kingly prerogative,[5] and was extended to the temple priesthood as

1. See vol.1, pp.114-118.
2. See vol.2, pp.158-161.
3. See vol.1, pp.143-145.
4. Notice that the address to the priests is indirect compared to the direct address to the entire congregation of Israel.
5. See ch.4 in conjunction with the discussion of "glory."

locum tenens of the king, came to be viewed in the post-exilic period as the prerogative of all members of the community. Put otherwise, the people *as immediate subjects of the divine King*, could address him in prayer directly, i.e., using the "kingly" pattern and phraseology.

Consequently, qualities that were essentially divine and kingly, such as *saddiq* and *hasid*, became qualifiers of the people *without* the intermediacy of the king. Appeal to God for rescue from sickness or other calamity is replete with reference to the wicked, the evil, foes, and enemies. Hence, it is extremely hard to decide for or against a pre- or post-exilic origin for many psalms on the basis of whether the personal pronouns are first or third person, or singular or plural. A psalmist who uses the word "I" may be the post-exilic individual Judahite rather than the king; one who uses the term "we" may be a pre-exilic king who is including his people in the petition, rather than a post-exilic Judahite speaking for all the people. These uncertainties explain why scholars are frequently divided in their judgment of the provenance of any given psalm. However, the burden of proof should lie with those who want to interpret a psalm as post-exilic, for the following reason: why would someone invent a completely new psalm for a given situation when it is much easier to modify one that already exists, is readily available, and uses similar terminology? It will have been worthwhile to create an entirely new psalm only when a particular exilic or post-exilic situation was so radically new that no existing psalm offered a reasonably good model or starting point. This view seems to be corroborated by the ascription of most of the psalms to pre-exilic personalities such as David,[6] (the sons of) Korah,[7] or Asaph.[8] Both of the latter were Levites (1 Chr 6:19-22; 39-43), i.e., in the temple service, while Asaph is specifically identified as a

---

6. Ps 3-41; 51-65; 68-70; 86; 101; 103; 108-110; 122; 124; 131; 133; 138-145. The Hebrew preposition *l* can mean either "to" or "for." In the latter instance, we have an even stronger case for the tradition having viewed the psalms as mostly royal.

7. Ps 42-43 (combined), 44-49; 84; 85; 87; 88.

8. Ps 50; 73-83.

temple musician (v.31). If we add to this list the fifteen psalms of ascent 120-134—among which are the "Davidic" psalms 122; 124; 131; 133—the conclusion is clear: the psalms were viewed as related to the temple service, and thus cultic in the strictest sense. This would apply only to a pre-exilic and *royal* setting.

As for the specifically post-exilic situations and circumstances, they all boil down to either the national catastrophe of the destruction of Jerusalem or its corollary, the demise of the kingly office. The first gave rise to Ps 74; 79; 137, and possibly 51.[9] The second had a much more varied spectrum of consequences, creating new focuses on the Law, wisdom, and history.

Exaltation of the Law

We saw in ch.6 how the kingly rule expressed the divine will insofar as it abided by the divine law. It is thus the law (*torah*) that, in the eventual elimination of the king as necessary intermediary between God and his people, became the *direct and immediate* bridge between the latter two; hence the preeminence of the *torah* in nascent Judaism.[10] This explains why all of Ps 119 is devoted to the subject of the divine law as post-exilic Judah's primary hope and the primary focus of its people's interest.[11] This psalm is arranged acrostically. The adjective "acrostic" derives from the Greek *akrostikhis* ("end-line," from *akron*, "extremity" and *stikhos,* "line, verse") and refers to poems written in such a way that the beginning letters of their verses (or sets of verses) spell out a word, a name, a sentence, or sometimes simply the alphabet. This last option is the method used for all of the acrostic psalms—9 and 10 (combined),[12] 25, 34, 37, 111, 112, 119 and 145. Ps 119 is unique in that it is composed of 22 sets of eight verses, corresponding to the 22

9. However, see Eaton, p.72.
10. See vol.1, pp.143-145 and vol.2, pp.160-161.
11. Compare with Ps 19 where the praise of the divine law (vv.7-13) forms a section of a royal psalm.
12. Which explains their numbering as one (Ps 9) in the Septuagint.

letters of the Hebrew alphabet; moreover, each of the eight verses in a given set starts with the same letter that governs the entire set.

Wisdom Psalms

Another consequence of the demise of kingship was the interest in wisdom, a quality specifically connected with the royal office.[13] A number of psalms are of a didactic nature (Ps 14//53; 49; 104), in which the psalmist speaks "universally" as a wisdom teacher would. However, it is precisely that "universal" tone that makes it possible, if not very probable, that the speaker might either be the king or at least be using royal phraseology.

Historical Psalms and the God of the Pentateuch

Another kind of didactic psalm is represented by 78; 105; 106; 135; and 136. These speak of the "story" of God and Israel and thus can more specifically be referred to as the "historical" psalms. Their exilic or post-exilic provenance can be assessed on the basis of the fact that their content basically follows the "story" recorded in the Pentateuch and the Deuteronomistic History. In other words, their viewpoint corresponds to that of nascent Judaism. The reality with which God is dealing directly is Israel, while kingship is handled only at the end of Ps 78 (vv.67-72) and in messianic terms similar to Ezek 34: David will "shepherd" forever Jacob/Israel, God's people/inheritance (Ps 78:70-71).

References to events other than the institution of kingship to describe God's relationship with his people did not constitute a novelty in themselves,[14] but here the entire "story" is presented exclusively from a Pentateuchal, i.e., non-kingly, viewpoint. In other words, the "story" itself in these Psalms actually replaces the pre-exilic institution of kingship; instead of loyalty to the king

13. See on this Part II on wisdom literature.
14. See e.g. Ps 95:7b-11; 99:6-8.

determining who is a part of God's people, it is adoption of this story as one's own that performs that function. At that earlier time, the deity was viewed by the people, and thus "defined" in their minds, within the parameters of ancient Near Eastern monarchy, in terms of the reality of the city-state, i.e., human civilization, which is tantamount to *human* accomplishment. The Pentateuchal deity, on the other hand, which is essentially the "exodus" deity, is defined within the parameters of the *midbar* (wilderness) which is the realm of desolation and death from the perspective of all communitarian existence, whether tribal or civilized in nature. In either case, life is sustained by water and agriculture, neither of which can be found in the *midbar*, where, purely and simply, there is no life or existence. In realistic terms, the *midbar* is for humans as forbidding a place as the chaotic waters: it is the impossible place, the non-place, the place where humans simply are not because they *cannot* be.

But it is precisely in terms of chaotic waters and wilderness that the Pentateuchal deity defines itself as well as its people "Israel." After having subdued the raging waters at the Red Sea, God establishes his reign on his holy mountain in the wilderness! And it is there, in the *midbar*, that he establishes, i.e., creates, his people by granting them his law. Through this law he establishes his king, and so the king's authority is not based on that of the city, which can be misunderstood to be as much the king's as God's. Rather, God criticizes and judges the king from his mountain in the wilderness. And the king he chooses to criticize is Solomon, the monarch par excellence:[15]

> When you come to the land which the Lord your God gives you, and you possess it and dwell in it, and then say, "I will set a king over me, like all the nations around me"; you may indeed set a king over you, him whom the Lord your God will choose...Only he must not multiply horses for himself, or cause the people to return to Egypt in order to multiply horses, since the Lord has said to you, "You shall not return

15. 1 Kg 3:4-10:25.

that way again." And he shall not multiply wives for himself, lest his heart turn away; nor shall he greatly multiply for himself silver and gold. (Deut 14-18)

That this is not an establishment of the monarchy, but rather a criticism of it, is corroborated by the fact that Solomon, we are told, does precisely those things which God forbade. To be sure, the basic account of Solomon's kingship is greatly praiseworthy. However, it is bracketed with the following remarks:

> So the kingdom was established in the hand of Solomon. Solomon made a marriage alliance with Pharaoh king of Egypt; he took Pharaoh's daughter, and brought her into the city of David...Solomon loved the Lord, walking in the statutes of David his father; only, he sacrificed and burnt incense at the high places.[16] (1 Kg 2:46-3:3)

> And Solomon gathered together chariots and horsemen...And the king made silver as common in Jerusalem as stone...And Solomon's import of horses was from Egypt...Now Solomon loved many foreign women: the daughter of Pharaoh...so Solomon did what was evil in the sight of the Lord, and did not follow the Lord as his father David had done...(1 Kg 10:26-11:6)

Reflections of this same point of view may be found in the historical psalms. Indeed, the history rendered in a historical psalm consisting of a limited number of verses is essentially identical to the long narrative extending across the eleven substantial books that form the Pentateuch and the Deuteronomistic History. This is a clear indication that history, as I showed in vol.1, ch.1, is not quantitative but qualitative. It is much more than an accumulation of interesting facts presented in chronological sequence; it is rather a chain of events essential to the self-understanding of the community ultimately based upon these events. It is actually the *chain* itself that forms the history. Indeed, an author of a multi-volume work on the history of a given country can be asked to write this same history as an encyclopedia article; and what makes this endeavor possible is that the two renderings basically follow the same *chain* of thought, i.e., of events. All that a more ample

16. Which is strictly forbidden by Deut 16:21-22.

rendition does, when compared to a shorter version, is to weave more details around each of the main events. Thus, the reference to Abraham in a historical psalm, for instance, epitomizes what this person means for the community; conversely, the Pentateuchal traditions regarding Abraham are an "exegesis" of the reality and meaning of this forefather for the same community that views itself as his progeny. The same applies to George Washington for the United States citizen: whether one spells out his name, or refers to him as the "father of the American nation," or writes an article or a book about him, all three endeavors boil down to stating what the reality reflected in these two words means for the United States citizen.

Depending on the point or points it intends to underscore, each of the historical psalms lists its own series of events that form the Pentateuchal story and the Deuteronomistic History. But these are just different perspectives of the same reality, as can be seen from the fact that they all follow the same sequence based on a well-established tradition:

1. Creation and God's creative power (Ps 135:5-7; 136:4-7).

2. Abraham, Isaac, and Jacob (Ps 105:6-15).

3. Joseph (Ps 135:16-22).

4. Jacob in Egypt (Ps 105:23-25).

5. Moses and Aaron (Ps 105:26-27).

6. The plagues against Egypt (Ps 78:42-51; 105:26-37).

7. The exodus (Ps 78:9-13, 53b; 105:38; 106:6-12; 135:8-9; 136:10-15).

8. The sojourn in the wilderness (Ps 78:14-16, 51-52a; 105:39-42; 136:16).

9. The rebellion against God and the people's chastisement by him (Ps 106:13-31).

10. The defeat of adverse kings on the way to Canaan (Ps 135:10-12; 136:17-22).

11. The entrance into Canaan (Ps 78:54-55; 105:43-45).

12. The people's disobedience in Canaan and the period of the Judges (Ps 78:56-59; 106:34-46)

13. The fall of Samaria (Ps 78:60-66).

14. The exile (Ps 106:47).

15. The Messianic era (Ps 78:67-72).

Each of the five psalms contains a reference to the exodus and to one or more features of the sojourn in the wilderness between the exodus and the entrance into Canaan. This corresponds to the Pentateuchal story where these two elements together occupy the lion's share of the text (the books of Exodus, Leviticus, Numbers, and Deuteronomy). This again confirms that in the post-exilic period, the cultic God addressed in Israel's prayers was none other than the Pentateuchal deity.

Anti-History

A striking feature in the historical psalms' handling of the two central events of exodus and sojourn in the wilderness, is that they are not presented as mere divine actions as a result of which Israel passively receives God's beneficence. Quite the opposite, Israel is very active—but its activity is negative! Not only does it consistently refuse to follow God's will, but it *actively opposes* what God himself does for it.[17] Time and again it reverses what God has accomplished, which ultimately amounts to its own birth as a nation. Israel rebels against its own creation! It continually rebels against God in the wilderness where there is no water or food, rebelling against its only source for these elements,[18] its sole fountain of life. As for God, he is stubbornly deaf to Israel's resistance[19] and resolutely tries to bring the nation into the realm

17. See especially Ps 78:9-11, 17-20, 22, 32, 36-37, 40-42, 56-58.
18. Ps 78:15-16 and 23-28.
19. Ps 78:21-24, 38-39.

of existence *in spite of itself.*[20] Yet, paradoxically, the same God who kept stubbornly sinful Israel alive in the wilderness, the domain of death, postponed the ultimate punishment, total destruction, until after Israel had reached Canaan, the realm of life and existence![21]

The message is clear: it is God's law, i.e., his will, that grants and secures communitarian life. Indeed, although it seems as though the city is merely the reality within which divine law is applicable, in actuality it is the latter that founds, builds, and maintains the existence of the city.[22] And if so, then it was by the law granted in the wilderness of Sinai that Israel was brought into existence and maintained, insofar as that happened as a direct result of Israel's obedience to it. But instead of the law, Israel sought food and water for its sustenance, forgetting that the former was brought down from heaven, the divine domain,[23] and the latter was made to gush out from a dead and barren rock.[24] These events should have been sufficient to prove that God alone was necessary for Israel's sustenance, and in fact it was necessary that he perform such miracles to prove that fact. For if God had destroyed Israel in the wilderness, that could—*would*—have been misinterpreted as though Israel merely succumbed in the wilderness to the lack of food and water. So God waited until Israel was settled as a nation, in a city-state, and there, in the domain of secure existence, he unleashed his anger against it, thus showing Israel and everyone else that it is he, and only he, who makes and breaks his people.

Thus, the biblical story is in no way the story of Israel—let alone its history—but the story of God. A story—or a history—is related through deeds; according to the biblical story, however,

20. See vol.2, pp.154-155, on Ezek 20.
21. Ps 78:59-66.
22. See ch.5.
23. Ps 78:23-25.
24. Ps 78:15-16.

had Israel's deeds been allowed to take their course, they would have nipped Israel in the bud, in which case there would have been no Israel and no story to tell about it.. It is rather God's deeds, which are anti-deeds from the human perspective,[25] that created the biblical story as we have it. This story tells us that life, human and any other kind of earthly life, proceeds *directly* from God, without any intermediary, be it vegetation, oasis, king, city, or temple. His kingship lies in his shepherding role.[26] And whoever has witnessed the activity of shepherds in the Near East will have noticed two things:

1) Shepherding takes place at the fringes of settled life, where wilderness, the domain of death and nonexistence, is daily experienced.

2) The flock is not an agglomeration of sheep, but rather a creation of the shepherd. Without him the sheep would scatter and ultimately perish. The existence of the individual sheep is literally bound to the reality we call a flock, and there is a flock only where there is a shepherd who walks *ahead* of the sheep that recognize the sounds emitted by him and who thus "follow his voice."

What applies to Israel applies also to Judah once it has entered into a covenant with the God of Israel.[27] It is no wonder then that Jeremiah's rejected oracle of destruction against Jerusalem and the temple (Jer 7:1-15; 26:1-11) was justified with the following words:

> Thus says the Lord of hosts, the God of Israel: "Add your burnt offerings to your sacrifices, and eat the flesh. For in the day that I brought them out of the land of Egypt, I did not speak to your fathers or command them concerning burnt offerings and sacrifices. But this command I gave them, '*Obey my voice*, and I will be your God, and you shall be my people; and walk in all the way that I command you, that it may be well with you.' But they did not *obey or incline their ear*, but

25. Since they work against the will of the people.
26. Ps 78:70-72. See also Ezek 34.
27. See vol.1, pp.23-26, 60.

walked in their own counsels and the stubbornness of their evil hearts, and went backward and not forward. From the day that your fathers came out of the land of Egypt to this day, I have persistently sent all my servants the prophets to them, day after day; yet they did not *listen to me, or incline their ear*, but stiffened their neck. They did worse than their fathers." (Jer 7:21-26)

Liturgy

That the recollection of God's deeds constitutes thanksgiving[28] and praise[29] to him is understandable. What is amazing, however, is that Old Testament psalmody also includes, in Ps 78, teaching material (see vv.1-4) consisting of a mere recitation of divine deeds.[30] Since this psalm essentially "defines" God and Israel for the congregation, it must be that this very act of definition became a necessary liturgical action in nascent Judaism. And it became necessary because the divine deeds and history that were to be remembered were in fact *anti*-deeds and *anti*-history, i.e., an impossibility from the human perspective. Whereas the simple appellation "God" or "Lord" was self-explanatory and thus sufficient in pre-exilic Jerusalem, where the deity was enthroned in the visible temple of a tangible nation, the anti-historical God of nascent Judaism had to be constructed time and again as a reality in the mind of the gathered congregation. This action was an absolute necessity because this congregation of Israel was itself a product of God in that it came into being against its own will. Without this definition of God there would be no congregation to begin with! Put otherwise, the recollection of the divine *anti*-deeds and Israel's stubborn resistance to them was the sine qua non condition, the basis for every prayer in nascent Judaism; in such recollection lay the definition and ultimately the very presence of both Israel's God and God's Israel.

28. Ps 105: 1; 106:1, 48; 136:1-3, 26.
29. Ps 105:2-3, 45; 106:1; 135:1-4, 19-21.
30. See also Ps 49 for this type of psalmody.

This explains the necessity of the anamnesis prayer in the two central gatherings of the Christian community, baptism and eucharist. It is in these liturgical services that the Christian individual and the church are defined—i.e., born, made, brought about—through God's grace and in spite of their stubbornly sinful will and deeds. The lengthy and defining anamnesis,[31] which is nothing but an overview of the divine deeds detailed in the Christian scripture of both Old and New Testaments, *makes present* the "biblical" God who consummated his *anti*-deeds, i.e., his being, in Jesus the Christ as expressed in the apostolic teaching of the New Testament. It is only at this point, i.e., after the Christian "biblical" God has been defined, *made present*, through the recitation of the "biblical" story as expressed in the "biblical" words, that the actual petition for the occasion, the sending of *that God's* Holy Spirit to enact *his* will, is uttered.

Our feelings and personal experience in this matter are totally irrelevant, if not detrimental. Since they are *ours*, all they are capable of producing is *our* conception of God, which is nothing than a figment of *our* imagination. In other words, feelings and personal experience produce a god that is part of *our* history, i.e., the story of *our* deeds, which is strictly a deity that is *our* construct. In the baptismal and eucharistic liturgies, however, we do not say "Amen" to *our understanding* of the words uttered by the celebrant but rather to the latter's *actual* words. (Imagine only the computerized image resulting from the mixture of the *individual* feelings and experiences of those gathered at that moment, and then imagine that this is the god you are praying to! At best, it will be that of a monster!) We say "Amen" and thus acquiesce to the *anti*-deed, the *grace*-ful action of the "biblical" God, i.e., the God who has just been defined through the "biblical" story uttered by the celebrant, *in spite of us and our feelings, imaginations, and experiences.* Consequently we are ourselves "born," "created,"

31. For the eucharist, my reader is referred to the Liturgy of St Basil the Great.

"made," "brought about" according to *his* will and after the image of *his* Son.

This means that the words and story of the liturgical anamnesis are not to be felt, but rather heard and *understood*:

> Give ear, O my people, to my *teaching* (*torati*, **torah**);
> incline your ears to the *words* (*'imre*, utterances) of my mouth!
> I will open my mouth in a parable;
> I will utter dark sayings (riddles) from of old,
> things that we have *heard and known,*
> that our fathers have *told* us.
> We will not hide them from their children,
> but *tell* to the coming generation
> the *glorious deeds* of the Lord, and his might,
> and the *wonders which he has wrought.* (Ps 78:1-4)

Hence the necessity and centrality of catechetical instruction in the early church, reflected in as early a document as Paul's first epistle to the Corinthians:

> I am thankful that I baptized none of you except Christus and Gaius; lest anyone should say that you were baptized in my name. (I did baptize also the household of Stephanas. Beyond that, I do not know whether I baptized any one else.) *For Christ did not send me to baptize but to preach the gospel,* and not with eloquent words, lest the cross of Christ be emptied of its power. (1 Cor 1:14-16)[32]

The Niceo-Costantinopolitan Creed

This tradition of teaching and understanding the faith ultimately led to the establishment of formulaic confessions of faith which all Christians were expected to adopt as their own. Such formulas, Christian versions of the historical psalms, were developed by the bishops and presbyters, the leaders of the Christian community whose main duty was preaching and teaching the tradition that originated with the apostles.[33] These expressions of faith composed

32. See also Acts 6:2-4.

33. 1 Tim 1:10; 4:4-6, 11, 13, 16; 5:17; 6:2-3, 20; 2 Tim 1:12-14; 2:2; 3:14-16; 4:3; Titus 1:9, 13; 2:1, 8.

by and for the one, holy, catholic, and apostolic church were codified at the first two ecumenical councils of Nicea (325 A.D.) and Constantinople (381), and the resulting creed has since become the primary expression of the faith of the church universal.[34] It not only renders the "biblical" story from beginning (creation) to end (the coming Kingdom), but does so almost exclusively with terminology taken directly from the Bible. In fact, the greatest controversy surrounding the formulation of that creed was over the inclusion in it of a single non-scriptural term, *homoousios* (of one [i.e., the same] essence),[35] to help describe the relationship between the Son of God and his Father. After lengthy debate, *homoousios* was accepted. But it was considered necessary to include around it an unusually large amount of additional explanatory phrases drawn directly from scripture, such as "son of God," "only-begotten," "light of light," "true God of true God," "by whom all things were made." In this context *homoousios* was intended to function not as a new revelation of who Jesus was but merely as an additional comment on the biblical language to ensure that it was understood correctly. All this is evidence of the church's awareness in those early centuries that its God was none other than the "biblical" God and as such *had to be expressed biblically,* i.e., using the same words as in the "biblical story" itself.

Since it is this creed that stands at the beginning of, i.e., as a condition for, both the baptismal and the eucharistic liturgies, every effort must be made to ensure that it is *understood* according to the faith of the one, holy, catholic, and apostolic church, and not according to any individual feelings and experiences. Such efforts cannot be directed solely at perfecting the verbal formulae of the creed itself, because no such formulae can be so perfect as to preclude misunderstanding. The key must be to *teach* people

---

34. It is endorsed by all Christian families since the first major schism that tore the Christian community apart took place 50 years later, at the ecumenical council of Ephesus in 431.

35. See Henry R. Percival, *The Seven Ecumenical Councils,* vol. XIV, second series, pp.3-4, in *The Nicene and Post-Nicene Fathers,* P. Schaff, ed.

the meaning intended to be expressed by the words; hence the lengthy period of catechumenate before baptism and the "liturgy of the catechumens" as a necessary preamble to the "liturgy of the faithful," *as necessary for the faithful themselves as for the catechumens.* The Baptismal Catecheses of Cyril, bishop of Jerusalem, witness to the importance of scripture in establishing the meaning of the words of the creed. They were first delivered in the fourth century after the Council of Nicea, and their subject matter clearly follows the order of the articles of the Nicene Creed, but the content of their teaching is scriptural through and through. The same is true of the "liturgy of the catechumens": it revolves around scriptural readings followed by explicative and exhortatory sermons on these readings. All of these practices of the Christian church are based on the same principles that led to the creation of the historical psalms.

8

The Psalter

Rereading of Pre-Exilic Psalms

Since nascent Judaism defined itself along the lines of its "first and second scriptures," i.e., the *torah* (Pentateuch) and the *nebi'im* (the Deuteronomistic History and the prophetic books),[1] for any other literature to be approved by Judaism it would have to conform to the mindset of these scriptures. In the case of the psalms this meant that they had to become Jewish prayers, and such was obviously not possible unless they were addressed to the God of Judaism. We have seen in the previous chapter that this was a comparatively easy matter in the majority of the cases; these were royal psalms that either sounded strictly personal or included the people in the petition. Each of these was read as the prayer of an individual *hasid* or *saddiq* who was petitioning on his own behalf as well as on behalf of his peers. Examples are psalms of distress, personal or collective, and psalms for relief from sickness. As for the psalms where the king or the Davidic dynasty is expressly mentioned, they were read in the vein of the Messianic, Davidic and Zionist oracles found especially in the books of Isaiah, Ezekiel, Micah, and Zechariah. In other words, they were read as referring to the eschatological Messiah.[2]

Within this tradition of Messianism two of the royal psalms, 2 and 110, were of particular interest and became the Messianic psalms par excellence. The reason is obvious: they both contain a direct address of God himself to the king and thus, when applied to the "expected/coming one," could easily be termed as divine "prophetic oracles." This in

1. See vol.1, pp.143-145 and vol.2, pp.203-205.

2. See on this vol.2, p.125.

turn explains their central role in the New Testament literature
where Jesus is viewed as the Messiah expected at the end of times
and foretold by the Old Testament prophecies.

The Ascription to David

Nascent Judaism's eschatology revolved around the "new" David
and the "new" Jerusalem, as can be seen more clearly in the two
books of Chronicles.[3] Here, although the Jerusalem temple was
not built until the reign of Solomon, the Chronicler views David
as the originator and architect of the organization of the temple
service.[4] This explains why most of the royal psalms were ascribed
to David, the king par excellence, although many were attributed
to—or actually composed by—temple servers.[5] In other words,
David became the "psalmist" and the Book of Psalms came to be
known as the Book of the Psalms "of David."[6]

Collections of Psalms

The Book of Psalms seems to be the last step in a process that
began with smaller collections. That such collections must have
existed can be gathered from the following features:

1) The existence of doublets.[7]

2) The exclusive use of *'elohim* (God) in one set of psalms[8] and
of *yahweh* (the Lord) in others.[9]

3) Series of psalms attributed to one author[10] or linked together with the same title.[11]

3. See vol.1, pp.147-149.
4. See vol.1, p.148.
5. See below.
6. See vol.2, p. 109.
7. Ps 53 and 14; Ps 70 and 40:13-17; Ps 108:1-5 and 57:8-12; Ps 108:6-13 and
   60:5-12.
8. Ps 42-89.
9. Ps 3-41 and Ps 90-150.
10. Sons of Korah (42-49); Asaph (Ps 73-83).
11. Song of ascent (Ps 120-134); Hallel or Praise (Ps 105-107; 111-118; 146-150).

The Book of Psalms

Each of Ps 41; 72; 89; and 106 ends with a stereotypical doxology that does not correspond to the content of the psalm it concludes:

> Blessed be the Lord, the God of Israel,
>   from everlasting to everlasting!
> Amen and Amen. (Ps 41:13)

> Blessed be the Lord, the God of Israel,
>   who alone does wondrous things.
> Blessed be his glorious name forever;
>   may his glory fill the whole earth!
> Amen and Amen! (Ps 72:18-19)

> Blessed be the Lord forever!
> Amen and Amen. (Ps 89:52)

> Blessed be the Lord, the God of Israel,
>   from everlasting to everlasting!
> And let all the people say, "Amen!"
> Praise the Lord! (Ps 106:48)

At the end of the entire book of Psalms, Ps 150 is a pure doxology where, after the opening "Praise the Lord! Praise God in his sanctuary," each subsequent colon begins with "Praise him..." These similar doxologies are a clear indication that the editors intended to divide the Psalms into five sections, very probably after the pattern of the *torah's* (Pentateuch's) division into five books. The reason may well have been liturgical: the Psalms could thus be read concurrently with the Pentateuch over a period of time.

When one considers that the liturgical cycle in Judaism included readings from the "second scripture," the *nebi'im*, alongside those of the "first scripture," the *torah*, then it stands to reason that the collection of the Psalter was patterned after that of the Deuteronomistic History (*nebi'im ri'šonim*) and the prophetic collection (*nebi'im 'aharonim*), as well as of each scroll in this collection (Isaiah, Jeremiah, Ezekiel, and the scroll of the twelve prophets).[12]

12. See on this matter vol.2, pp.144-145, 161, 197-198, 201-205.

In other words, the editing of the Psalter followed the pattern of the "story of the biblical God."

Indeed, the first two collections (Ps 3-41 and 42-72) contain psalms overwhelmingly attributed to David. That this is intentional can be gathered from the last verse of Ps 72: "The prayers of David, the son of Jesse, are ended." (v.20) Whereas the first collection comprises exclusively "Davidic" psalms, the second includes also the work of the sons of Korah (Ps 42-49) and of Asaph (Ps 50). The third collection (Ps 73-89) is basically divided between these two: the latter is assigned Ps 73-83 and the former, Ps 84, 84, 87, and 88. On the other hand, the first collection is "yahwistic," the second and third—"elohistic." The last two collections (Ps 90-106 and 107-150) are "yahwistic" and are basically comprised of the "Songs of Ascent" (Ps 120-134) sandwiched between two sets of *hallel* (Praise) psalms (105-107 plus 11-118, and 135-136 plus 146-150).

I strongly believe the "story of the biblical God" in the Psalter runs in the following way. Book I covers the beginnings of the Davidic reign where Yahweh, the deity of Zion, was ruling[13] through his elect David, God's vassal par excellence.[14] Book II deals with the latter period of David's reign and the post-David Judahite kingdom up to the destruction of Jerusalem. The deity is referred to mainly as *'elohim* (God), which seems to reflect the gradual abandonment of the strict allegiance to Yahweh represented by David. This is enhanced by the following:

1) The start of the collection is made up of non-Davidic psalms. This can be taken either positively or negatively. In the former case, it would reflect the tradition that considered David as the founder of the temple service. In the latter instance, which is more probable, it would be a sign of the rejection of David as the Lord's only high priest.

13. The psalms of Book I are exclusively "yahwistic."
14. See vol.1, p.148; vol.2, pp.125, 139, 159.

2) The Davidic section of Book II begins with Ps 51, a psalm of penitence which the editors attributed to David's contrition after his adultery with Bathsheba and the murder of Uriah. These are considered to be the sins by which David incurred the Lord's wrath which ultimately led to the final catastrophe of 587.[15]

3) The last psalm (72) of the Davidic section is ascribed to Solomon, which can hardly be coincidental. According to the Deuteronomistic Historian, the long process that ultimately led to the catastrophe of exile originated in Solomon's reign, and specifically it began because of his neglect of the kingly duties delineated in this psalm.

Book III reflects the exilic setting:

1) It is mainly "elohistic." The deity of Zion, which Judah rejected, proves to be, as *'elohim* (God), universal and thus capable of chastising its people by exiling them among the nations; yet it also keeps an eye on the chastised people in order to redeem them at the opportune moment.[16]

2) The lack of hope is reflected in the "absence" of David: except for Ps 86, all of the psalms are non-Davidic.

3) When it is time to announce the return of hope, in Ps 86 the editors allow the voice of David to resound as the "servant of the Lord" (vv.2 and 4) who cries to God for help and fully trusts that he will answer. Moreover, David's prayer is preceded by the people's supplication for restoration (Ps 85) and followed by a petition for Zion to be (re-)established (Ps 87), a situation which parallels the setting of Second Isaiah.

4) The last psalm (89) is a cry of faith in the Lord who has hidden himself to punish those who rejected him and yet will remember the oath he made to David. With this, Book III ends on a tone of hope characteristic of Ezekiel and Second Isaiah.

15. See 2 Sam 12:11-12.

16. See Ezekiel and Second-Isaiah on this matter (vol.2, pp.149-166).

5) This feeling of hope is also reflected in the fact that after starting with the "elohistic" psalms 73-83, the collection shifts to addressing Yahweh in Ps 85-89 following the transition psalm 84 which uses both "Yahweh" and "God" equally. Since the last two collections are almost entirely "yahwistic,"[17] it seems likely that this transition was deliberately planned, the purpose being to present Yahweh, the deity of Zion (to be restored) as taking over from here on, in order to implement his eschatological rule.

Book IV, which reflects the end of the exilic period, appropriately starts with the only psalm (90) ascribed to Moses, the man of exodus. The psalm ends with this note:

> Return, O Lord! How long?
>> Have pity on thy servants! ...
>> Let thy work be manifest to thy servants,
>> and thy glorious power to their children.
>> Let the favor of the Lord our God be upon us,
>> and establish thou the work of our hands upon us,
>>> yea, the work of our hands establish thou it. (vv.13, 16-17)

At the end of the collection we have two "historical" and *hallel* psalms, 105 and 106. Their structure is interesting in that both recall the exodus, yet Ps 105 ends with the original gift of the land (vv.43-45) while Ps 106 refers to the exile (vv.40-46) and prays for the return to the land (v.47). In between the beginning psalm and the end psalms, and thus at the heart of this hope for the end of the exile, stands the lengthy series of psalms in honor of Yahweh the King (93, 95-100), which again harks back to the views of Ezekiel and Second Isaiah.

That the end of the exile is brought about by the promise connected with the "new Jerusalem"[18] can be seen in the smooth transition from Book IV to Book V. The latter opens with Ps 107 which with Pss 105 and 106 forms a triad of *hallel* psalms. The "elohistic" psalm 108 follows. Its placement at this juncture is

17. Except for Ps 108.

18. See again Ezekiel and Second Isaiah as well as the book of Jeremiah.

probably intentional because it proclaims the redeemer Yahweh as the sole universal deity.[19] The ascription of Ps 108-110 to David also suggests a Second- and Third-Isaianic "mood" of Messianic hope or realization. In the new Jerusalem and under the leadership of the eschatological David are intoned the *hallel* psalms 111-118. Moreover, the new Jerusalem bears the name of "The Lord is there"[20] because it is entirely under the aegis of the Lord's law, to which is dedicated the lengthy psalm 119. It is toward this new Jerusalem that the community is invited to "go up" in the "Songs of Ascent" (Ps 120-134); here again, the anti-Solomonic criticism can be seen in the ascription to Solomon of Ps 127 which opens with the warning: "Unless the Lord builds the house, those who build labor in vain. Unless the Lord watches over the city, the watchman stays awake in vain." It is finally in this new Jerusalem that the Lord is praised in the *hallel* psalms 135-136 by those who never allowed themselves to forget Zion, Yahweh's city (Ps 137), those at whose head stands (the new) David to whom are ascribed Ps 138-145. Under his leadership the new community will praise the Lord forever in the ending *hallel* psalms 146-150. And the entire creation will join in the Lord's praise[21] *because* "He has raised up a horn for his people" (Ps 148:14).[22]

My interpretation of the structure of the Book of Psalms seems to be corroborated by the two opening and untitled psalms that function as an introduction to the entire Psalter. Ps 1 exalts the *saddiq* (righteous one), the Lord's servant who does not have dealings with the *reša'im* (wicked), the Lord's enemies, because he abides by the Lord's *torah* (law), the expression of the divine will. Ps 2 is the kingly psalm par excellence, but it is at the same time messianic. It points out that the Lord will realize his promise to

19. See vol.2, pp.164-165 on Second Isaiah.
20. Ezek 48:35.
21. Ps 148:1-12.
22. On this issue see my comments on the Deutero-Isaianic *'ebed* poems in vol.2, pp.166-185.

those who trust in him (the righteous ones of Ps 1) through his *saddiq* par excellence, the "new David," who will implement, as only a perfect king would, the divine *torah*. That these two psalms are tightly connected can be seen in the fact that the first opens with "Blessed is the man (*'ašre ha'iš*) ... whose delight is in the law of the Lord, and on his law he meditates day and night" (vv.1:1a, 2), while the second closes with "Blessed are all (*'ašre kol*) who take refuge in him" (v.2:11c), as only a (perfect) king would.[23] This is an appropriate introduction to a book of eschatological prophecy, and that is precisely what I am convinced the Psalter was meant to be. The book as a whole is an attempt to reprise, in a liturgical manner, the *torah-nomos* (Law) and the *nebi'im-prophetai* (Prophets) in order to present the "story of the biblical God" which can only end by pointing to the future.[24]

---

23. The expression "take refuge in the Lord" is a recurrent and virtually exclusive feature of the royal psalms: Ps 5:11; 7:1; 11:1; 16:1; 17:7; 18:2, 30; 25:20; 31:1, 19; 36:7; 37:40; 57:1 (twice); 61:4; 64:10; 71:1; 91:4; 118:8, 9; 141:8;

24. The use of the Psalter as a book of prophecy is evident in the Lukan writings: Lk 20:41-43; 24:44; Acts 1:15-16, 20; 13:32-33, 35.

II

Wisdom Literature

9

Wisdom

The vital importance of wisdom in ancient Near Eastern life and thought can be seen in the following classic passage found in the works of both the Deuteronomistic Historian and the Chronicler:

And the king went to Gibeon to sacrifice there, for that was the great high place; Solomon used to offer a thousand burnt offerings upon that altar. At Gibeon the Lord appeared to Solomon in a dream by night; and God said, "Ask what I shall give you." And Solomon said, "Thou hast shown great and steadfast love to thy servant David my father, because he walked before thee in faithfulness, in righteousness, and in uprightness of heart toward thee; and thou hast kept for him this great and steadfast love, and hast given him a son to sit on his throne this day. And now, O Lord my God, thou hast made thy servant king in place of David my father, although I am but a little child; I do not know how to go out or come in. And thy servant is in the midst of thy people whom thou hast chosen, a great people, that cannot be numbered or counted for multitude. Give thy servant therefore an understanding mind to govern thy people, that I may discern between good and evil; for who is able to govern this thy great people?"

It pleased the Lord that Solomon asked this. And God said to him, "Because you have asked this, and have not asked for yourself long life or riches or the life of your enemies, but have asked for yourself understanding to discern what is right, behold, I now do according to your word. Behold, I give you a wise and discerning mind, so that none like you has been before you and none like you shall arise after you. I give you also what you have not asked, both riches and honor, so that no other king shall compare with you, all your days. And if you will walk in my ways, keeping my statutes and my commandments, as your father David walked, then I will lengthen your days."

And Solomon awoke, and behold, it was a dream. Then he came to Jerusalem, and stood before the ark of the covenant of the Lord, and offered up burnt offerings and peace offerings, and made a feast for all his servants. (1 Kg 3:4-15//2 Chr 1:3-12; see also 1 Kg 10:8-9)

Here we are told that the king, the guarantor of life in the city, the typical societal unit in the ancient Near East, dispenses *mišpat*, the basis for this life,[1] through the medium of wisdom. That this wisdom is granted by God and is thus divine (1 Kg 3:28) should come as no surprise since according to Prov 8:22-31 God himself, a "kingly" being, rules and orders his kingdom, the world, through the intermediacy of this same wisdom. The fact that divine and kingly wisdom amount to one and the same thing is clear from Proverbs where wisdom says: "By me kings reign, and rulers decree what is just; by me princes rule, and nobles govern the earth." (8:15-16)

Yet it is at the outset of this same chapter which speaks of wisdom in such lofty terms, that we read:

Does not wisdom call,
   does not understanding raise her voice?
On the heights beside the way,
in the paths she takes her stand;
beside the gates in front of the town,
at the entrance of the portals she cries aloud;
"To you, O men, I call,
and my cry is to the sons of men.
O simple ones, learn prudence;
O foolish men, pay attention." (vv.1-5)

Here divine/kingly wisdom is presented as attainable by ordinary human beings—men/sons of men/simple ones/foolish men—i.e., by *everyone*. Nor is this the only place where such wide distribution is deemed possible. Actually, the first time one encounters wisdom personified, at the outset of the Book of Proverbs purportedly written by "Solomon, the son of David, king of Israel," we are told:

Wisdom cries aloud in the street;
   in the markets she raises her voice;
on the top of the walls she cries out;
at the entrance of the city gates she speaks:

1. See ch.3.

"How long, O simple ones, will you love being simple?
How long will scoffers delight in their scoffing
and fools hate knowledge?
Give heed to my reproof;
behold, I will pour out my thoughts to you;
I will make my words known to you." (1:20-23)

How can it be that the wisdom which is essentially divine or kingly is at the same time in the immediate reach of every one, right there in the commonest, least exclusive place in the life of humans—the city gates?

The City Gates

The *še'arim* (gates) in the ancient Near Eastern cities correspond to the *agora* of the Greek and Hellenistic city, the square of the medieval town, the green of our towns and villages, the *centrum* of modern European cities, or the downtown of the American cities. The *še'arim*, or its singular *ša'ar* (gate), refers to the area where people congregated to make the transactions necessary for their life, i.e., commerce. And, as is usually the case with human beings, any encounter includes an oral give-and-take, an exchange of thoughts. It is no wonder then that the *agora* was also the meeting place of the city political body as well as the arena where philosophers entertained their debates; New Testament readers are familiar with the episode in the Book of Acts that speaks of Paul's sojourn at Athens:

> Now while Paul was waiting for them at Athens, his spirit was provoked within him as he saw that the city was full of idols. So he argued in the synagogue with the Jews and the devout persons, and in the market place every day with those who chanced to be there. Some also of the Epicurean and stoic philosophers met him. And some said, "What would this babbler say?" Others said, "He seems to be a preacher of foreign divinities"—because he preached Jesus and the resurrection. And they took hold of him to the Areopagus,[2] saying, "May we know what this new teaching is which you present?" (17:16-19; see also 16:19)

2. A hilly site at the southern end of the Athenian agora.

Speaking at the agora (market place) allowed Paul to reach the Athenians, in effect the *entire* city of Athens. This same value and meaning of the agora applies to the square or green: it is the spot that serves as a market place and an area for political gatherings. This is still the case in some villages and small towns in Switzerland, where the entire electoral body meets to discuss and vote on issues pertaining to the economic and socio-political life of the community.

When one considers that most of the ancient Near Eastern cities were much smaller than fortresses of the European Middle Ages, and thus were without streets as we know them today, then one will realize that the area of the city gate was the *only* place where citizens and visitors could congregate; literally, the entire life of the city took place at the city gates. That is why the palace/temple complex was usually adjacent to the gate area which then served as the temple court. Hence, by "entire life of the city," I mean the socio-political as well as the religious life; all communal life took place literally "in sight of" the king and/or deity, the "father" of the city and its inhabitants. In other words, the city gate wrapped up into one place what the living room, the back-yard, the bus or subway, the work place, the lounge, the bar, the restaurant, the park, the golf course, the church, the church hall, etc., are for a contemporary North American. Besides working in the fields surrounding the city, any citizen could be located during waking hours at the city gate. (1 Sam 9:18; 2 Sam 3:27; 15:2; Ruth 4:1, 9; Job 29:7-10) There, transactions and agreements were made (2 Kg 7:1, 18), and witnesses for them were readily available (Ruth 4:10-11). To secure as full an audience as possible, Jeremiah delivered his speeches at the city gates. (Jer 7:2; 17:19; 19:2; 26:10; 36:10) Sooner or later, one's name—equivalent to one's person in Hebrew thought—is bound to reach the city gates (Ruth 3:11;[3] Prov 31:31), and it tarries there throughout the years (Ruth 4:10). In modern terminology, the dilemma of "to be or

---

3. The Hebrew reads: "all the people at the gate" instead of "all my fellow townsmen."

not to be" is settled once and for all at the city gates. Finally, at the gates took place judicial decisions (2 Sam 15:2; Prov 22:22-23; Am 5:10, 12, 15; Zech 8:16) and similar actions of judgment and justice, essential functions of the divine/kingly ruler requiring wisdom. Hence, "Wisdom is too high for a fool; in the gate he does not open his mouth." (Prov 24:7)

The Elders

At the gates not everyone is equally wise. Justice and wisdom are preeminently attributed to the *zeqenim* (elders), the aged with gray hair, as is clear from the following texts:

> Wisdom is with the aged,
> and understanding in length of days. (Job 12:12)

> Are you the first man that was born?
> Or were you brought forth before the hills?
> Have you listened in the council of God?
> And do you limit wisdom to yourself?
> What do you know that we do not know?
> What do you understand that is not clear to us?
> Both the gray-haired and the aged are among us,
> older than your father. (Job 15:7-10)

> Stand in the assembly of the elders.
> Who is wise? Cleave to him. (Sir 6:34)

> You have gathered nothing in your youth;
> how then can you find anything in your old age?
> What an attractive thing is judgment in gray-haired men,
> and for the aged to possess good counsel!
> How attractive is wisdom in the aged,
> and understanding and counsel in honorable men!
> Rich experience is the crown of the aged,
> and their boast is the fear of the Lord. (Sir 25:3-6)

> Speak, you who are older,
> for it is fitting that you should. (Sir 32:3a)

This explains Elihu's reticence and belated intervention in the Book of Job:

Now Elihu had waited to speak to Job because they were older than he.
And when Elihu saw that there was no answer in the mouth of these
three men, he became angry. And Elihu the son of Barachel the Buzite
answered:

> "I am young in years,
>> and you are aged;
>> therefore I was timid and afraid
>> to declare my opinion to you." (Job 32:4-7)

This de facto equivalence between age and wisdom can best be
seen in a classical feature of wisdom literature: the addressee is
always called "son." The direction of the instruction is in one
sense from a father to his son and, by extension, from an elder to
a youth. It is as though only a father or an elder, never a son or a
youth, is able to bestow wisdom. And even when the point made
is that wisdom can be shared by a young person, "understanding"
is said to be tantamount to "gray hair":

> The glory of young men is their strength,
>> but the beauty of old men is their gray hair. (Prov 20:29)

In other words, in order to express the notion of wisdom/under-
standing, the imagery of "gray hair" comes to mind, i.e., a wise
man is always an "elder":

> For old age is not honored for length of time,
>> nor measured by number of years;
>> but understanding is gray hair for men,
>> and a blameless life is ripe old age. (Wis 4:8-9)

Wisdom and Folly

A striking feature of wisdom is that it is a reality in and of itself
and thus cannot be qualified. One does not speak of right versus
wrong wisdom, correct versus incorrect wisdom, good versus bad
wisdom, etc. One rather speaks of wisdom versus lack thereof. Put
otherwise, wisdom is wisdom or it is nothing at all. Its opposite is
folly or foolishness, which in turn is a reality in and of itself that
cannot be qualified. Where there is wisdom, there is no folly; and
vice versa, where there is folly wisdom is not to be found. A wise

man is not foolish, and a fool is unwise.[4] If this is so, then the knowledge, intelligence, and understanding that go hand in hand with wisdom are ipso facto right and correct, i.e., cannot in any way be shown to be wrong or incorrect. The reason is that a wise utterance or statement is done at the culmination of a long period of time during which its correctness has already been proven through a lengthy series of tests; if at any point in time an utterance or statement will have been proven wrong then it is folly, not wisdom. Wisdom is an outcome that has already been tested and shown to be right, it is already assertive reality, incontrovertible matter of fact. Wisdom is either accepted or refused, and whoever refuses it does nothing else except reveal his true identity as a fool. Hence the extreme statement:

> Crush a fool in a mortar with a pestle,
>   along with crushed grain,
>   yet his folly will not depart from him. (Prov 27:22)

The Universality of Wisdom

This incontrovertibility of wisdom can be understood only if one realizes that wisdom is basically universal. A given saying cannot be wisdom here and folly there; if it could, then it would be concomitantly wisdom and folly, which is an impossibility. Solomon was not wise in Israel and potentially a fool somewhere else. Rather:

> And God gave Solomon wisdom and understanding beyond measure, and largeness of mind like the sand on the seashore, so that Solomon's wisdom surpassed the wisdom of all the people of the East, and all the wisdom of Egypt. for he was wiser than all other men, wiser than Ethen the Ezrahite, and Hemen, Calcol, and Darda, the sons of Mahol; and his fame was in all the nations round about. He also uttered three thousand proverbs; and his songs were a thousand and five. He spoke of trees, from the cedar that is in Lebanon to the hyssop that grows out

4. Prov 1:7b; 10:8, 14; 12:15-16, 23; 13:16; 14:3, 8, 18, 24, 29; 15:2, 5, 14, 21; 16:22; 26:5; 29:9; Eccl 10:12.

of the wall; he spoke also of beasts, and of birds, and of reptiles, and of fish. And men came from all peoples to hear the wisdom of Solomon, and from all the kings of the earth, who had heard of his wisdom. (1 Kg 4:29-34)

Now when the queen of Sheba heard of the fame of Solomon concerning the name of the Lord, she came to test him with hard questions...and Solomon answered all her questions; there was nothing hidden from the king which he could not explain to her...And she said to the king: "... Happy are these your servants, who continually stand before you and hear your wisdom! Blessed be the Lord your God, who has delighted in you and set you on the throne of Israel! Because the Lord loved Israel for ever, he has made you king, that you may execute justice and righteousness." (1 Kg 10:1-9)

If, then, we place an adjective of locality before wisdom—such as Chinese wisdom, Indian wisdom, Greek wisdom—we cannot mean by that a kind of wisdom valid solely in that place. It simply means that those specific wisdom sayings were developed in that area; their value, however, is universal.[5] Witness thereof is the publication in contemporary Europe and America of books comprising wisdom sayings from different parts of the world as well as widely varying time frames: ancient Persia, ancient India, ancient China, Muslim civilization, different European countries, etc. The intention is clearly to impart a universal "wisdom" to the contemporary European and American readers.

The Time and Space Factor

The experience connected with wisdom is thus not narrowly individual, and that is why wisdom is not merely a feature of an elder but more precisely of an "elder at the gate." It is not enough to have lived a long time in order to acquire wisdom. One must actively "learn" it, "be instructed" in it. Otherwise, if "wisdom" is

---

5. The same, by the way, applies to fables that can be considered as part of wisdom literature. The lessons intended by the Greek fables of Aesop are definitely not valid only in ancient Greece. The proof is that they were taken over by the seventeenth century French writer La Fontaine and continue to be used in 20th century America.

learned only through common life experiences, through a process of trial and error, much of what one "acquires" will be folly rather than wisdom, until future experiences—which may never come—prove it otherwise. Thus, the time spent by an elder *at the gate* will have allowed him to be instructed by *other elders* who will have imparted unto him the knowledge they have learned from one another as well as from the visitors and merchants from other cities they have met at the city gates. Without this broader perspective, "wisdom" would be local, which is a contradiction in terms.

The city gate, as a modern-day university would, actually functioned as a microcosm, a place where the entire world, with its experience, knowledge, and wisdom were made readily available. There, in this universe in a nutshell as the city gate really was, was imparted "wisdom"—universal wisdom—whatever the point of origin of a given expression of it might have been.

The Council of Elders

The communal nature of wisdom as it was understood in the ancient Near East is further reflected in the fact that we almost never hear about individual elders in the Old Testament but rather of elders in the plural. The individual elder, insofar as such a person exists, is defined as one who is seated among the elders (Prov 31:23). The elders were not thus a plurality of individual elders; rather, the elder was a member of the council of elders. The tangible reality was ultimately the council or assembly, and not the individual member of it. Actually, whoever is a member of the council is an elder regardless of his age, whereas an old man, wise as can be, is not necessarily an "elder," in the strict sense, i.e., a council member. This same reality can still be perceived in our contemporary societies. For instance, in the USA, one speaks of Congress, Senate, and House of Representatives. We define a senator as a member of the Senate rather than speak of the Senate as being formed out of senators. Also, it is the vote of the Senate or the House that counts ultimately, not that of the senators or representatives. The latter do not rule; it is Congress that does. Another example can be seen in the institution of the jury: at the end of a jury's deliberation the judge asks it for its verdict, not of its constitutive members (except perhaps afterwards to verify that all concur in the verdict proclaimed as unanimous). It is the *one* voice of the judicial assembly that is decisive.

The Nature of Wisdom

But then, what is it that makes wisdom a similar matter and not one of opinion? Why must wisdom speak with one collective voice? If even in science one can still live with differing opinions, why must any disagreement with wisdom be considered folly? The answer is simple: wisdom's field of interest is the preservation of the flow of human life and of life on earth. Wisdom wants to make sure that the "foolish" alternative to life does not even get tested. Indeed, ultimately it cannot be tested, since who would be around to see and judge the effects of a test to see how the lack of life would look like? In order to secure the continued flow of life, one must first and foremost observe and learn to accommodate. To give an example: if wisdom literature includes a saying exhorting humans to learn assiduity from ants, it is not because it is interested in the science of insects, or in the ethics of work, or to combat the vice of slothfulness. The intention is rather to remind humans that food is essential for the preservation of human life, and that food must be procured, and stored for days when it cannot be procured. For us to still be around tomorrow, we had better extract for ourselves a lesson from the ants' behavior.

The necessity of wisdom is linked to the fact that humans are the only beings capable of altering the flow of life on our planet to the extent of extinguishing it. The other beings seem to instinctively follow the lead of life. Only man, with his ability of discursive thinking, is able to objectify life, to make out of it an object, an "it," and thus subject it to himself—and in doing so he forces it to follow his lead instead of himself following its lead. Wisdom works precisely on that level specific to humans, the level of discursive thought. It tries to express in discourse what life is, what our *entire* existence on this planet is all about; and it does so in order to preserve this life and thus allow it to continue. Why? Because the alternative is non-existence.

This explains why the origin of wisdom tradition lies in tribal communal life, where life itself is held by a very thin thread. In order to protect that thread, the "wise" authority of the tribal "father" and his council of elders is needed. "Authority" alone is not good enough; it must be *wise* authority because in the constant struggle to preserve life, the trial and error method is not allowed. "Error" is no alternative; error leads directly to disaster and destruction. By the same token, wisdom alone without authority is of no use because if its advice goes unheeded, the thread of life may break and there will be no chance to correct the error. So wisdom by its nature can only be authoritative and incontrovertible.

This concern of wisdom, the preservation of life, is not covered by any other science or philosophy. We only imagine that it is because we are the heirs of classical Greek philosophy which parted ways with ancient Near Eastern wisdom the moment it wanted to encompass under its wings all areas of human knowledge. And since such an endeavor is impossible, "philosophy" was bound to break down into philosophy and science, and then each of them into so many subjects, to the extent that many contemporary "philosophers," or rather students of philosophy, wonder if one can still speak at all of philosophy in the traditional sense. But wisdom in the ancient Near Eastern sense—as opposed to its common understanding today as an expression of individual experience—is still alive and well, or at least it had better be. We actually use it without naming it.

An example can be found in the contemporary debates regarding nuclear armament and the environment: any concern about such topics would be irrelevant if we—or our progeny or anyone else for that matter—will not be around because life on our planet has ceased to exist. Without even realizing it, those engaged in those debates are using the ways of wisdom by consistently warning us against the "alternative" of annihilation and non-existence.

It is clear, then, that wisdom is not an essentially religious matter. It is not specifically Christian and it is not linked even to belief in a monotheistic God. This is evident from the fact that many oriental religions, to whom that belief is foreign, have wisdom at the heart of their concern. Whether one refers to our world as "creation" in order to affirm the belief in a creator, or "nature" in order to deny such a belief, the laws and rules governing the universe are the same, be they physical, chemical, astronomical, biological, or whatever. Belief in a personal deity does not—or at least should not—influence scientific research into these laws and rules; such belief may affect our discussion of how what we learn from science is to be used and applied, but not its actual study.

Therefore, it is *wiser* and thus more profitable to consider that wisdom is basically human, as I showed earlier. Insisting that it is also divine is ultimately detrimental to any dialogue since it introduces a useless factor. The reason is simple: wisdom is wisdom, and whether it is considered divine or human, its field of interest is the same, since the laws and rules governing our universe, whether created by a deity or inherent, are not going to change.

Wisdom, King, and God

On the other hand, it was logical for wisdom in the ancient Near East to become especially associated with the king or the deity. Since the organizational character of the tribe is basically that of the biological family, wisdom tradition was a "natural" phenomenon: the father was ipso facto the elder and thus instructed his son, the youth, in the matters pertaining to life. The father's authority was readily accepted and did not need authentication by a higher authority such as the deity. For an entire clan or tribe, the leadership was constituted by all the elders rather than by only one; hence the council of elders, which was also a "natural" institution, i.e., in no need of either justification or authentication. With the rise of cities, the basic issue remained the same: securing life through communal order.[6] Here too wisdom was needed, but like many other traditions the terminology remained the same while the realities changed. In the city setting, wisdom terminology acquired an artificial, and thus forced, character. The king, whatever his age or experience, was the "father" of the people and its chief "elder." And although he was surrounded by a council, he could disregard it (1 Kg 12:6-11), which would have been impossible for a tribal chieftain who was bound by the unwritten rule of unanimity.[7] The king became more like a contemporary corporation CEO exercising autocratic authority, rather than a chairman who may lead but ultimately is first among equals. This "artificial" leadership required authentication, which was secured by a decree of the deity, who was believed to be the actual leader of the city.[8] Hence the notion that wisdom was granted to the king by the deity as well as the corollary that wisdom was ultimately divine. Thus, the king, by virtue of his office, had the wisdom which he needed to rule by.

Wisdom and the Law

The "artificiality" of the city as compared to the tribe required that, along with wisdom which was intangible, the deity would also grant the king a tangible expression of its will, and for this

6. See on this ch.1.
7. See above and also ch.1.
8. See Ps 2:7. See also my vol.2, pp.117 and 159.

reason what used to be oral tradition became written law.[9] Thus, wisdom on the one hand and law on the other became divine gifts to the king to rule the kingdom, the means by which the deity itself ruled its world. More precisely, the law with which the king was commissioned contained the specific guidelines along which the divine *mišpat* (justice/judgment) was to be implemented, which in turn secured the order necessary to preserve the flow of life. Wisdom was the personal quality of understanding and knowledge that ensured the law would be put to its intended purpose. In other words, whenever a king ascended the throne he would be entrusted with the divine law and the responsibility to uphold it, and he would be granted the wisdom with which to do that correctly. The simple authority that the tribal leader, or rather the tribal council of elders, exercised naturally could not survive in the setting of a city, where it developed into a trinitarian hierarchy: deity-law-king or, correspondingly, deity-wisdom-king.

Is there complete correspondence between these two hierarchical lines? The answer is negative. The first is really a hierarchy while the second is not. The deity is not, technically speaking, bound by the law whereas the king is. The law is a document expressing the deity's will: the deity rules its world according to its own unwritten will, while the king rules his kingdom by the deity's law. Wisdom, on the other hand, is a (divine) quality that the deity imparts to, and thus, shares with, the king. Whereas deity and king both rule with wisdom, it is only the king, strictly speaking, who rules by the law. Put otherwise, wisdom is necessary for both deity and king, whereas the law is necessary only for the king.

---

9. See ch.5. Actually the oldest ancient Near Eastern legal codes began as compilations of laws already extant and in usage.

10

The Post-Exilic Period

When the hopes of the Deuteronomistic Reform were shattered,[1] and Jeremiah's predictions prevailed,[2] and Jerusalem fell to the Babylonians in 587 B.C., for Judah the "artificial" society of the city collapsed and with it the hierarchy deity-law-king was proven ineffectual. The exilic priestly leaders, under Ezekiel's lead, looked back to the pre-monarchical period to build a model of a new Jerusalem that would not fall into the same predicament as the pre-exilic Davidic Jerusalem. They went all the way back to the "desert" where there are oases, not cities, i.e., where the deity was more of a tribal "father" and there was no king who by ignoring his deity's law could bring his entire city to ruin. They conceived a Mosaic *torah* given to the people without the intermediacy of the king, a law that was *the* Law, formulated in a way that gave rise to the Pentateuch, the incarnation of the Law.[3] This Law was not bound to a king, and thus not to a city either, and could therefore be implemented anywhere God's people was gathered as an *'edah* (synagogue). This was the practical expression of nascent Judaism.[4] But the priests' mentality is essentially linked to a temple,[5] and a temple is bound to a city; hence the centrality of a "Jerusalem," albeit a "new" one,[6] and of a David (the king), albeit a new one,[7] in the prophetic literature.[8] This is understandable since this

1. See vol.1, p.121.
2. See vol.1, p.124 and vol.2, pp.136-138.
3. See vol.1, pp.143-145 and vol.2, pp.160-161.
4. See vol.1, p.144.
5. See e.g. Ezek 40-48.
6. See e.g., Is 52:1-9; 62:1-7; 66:10-11, 20.
7. See e.g. Is 9:7, 11:1; Jer 23:5; 30:9; Ezek 34:23-24; 37:24-25.
8. See vol.2, pp.158-161 and 197-198.

literature made up the second part of the *nebi'im* (the second scripture) whose first part comprised the Deuteronomistic History. Whereas the latter was basically critical of pre-exilic Jerusalem, the former was critical of it too but at the same time suggestive of ways in which a "new" Jerusalem could correct the faults of the old one.[9]

Wisdom vs. Law

This prophetic literature points toward hope for an eschatological Jerusalem, one that could not possibly be prey to a mishandling of the law that would bring its destruction.[10] Such a Jerusalem could only be ruled by an equally eschatological king under whose leadership life and universal order would be ensured by a faultless implementation of the divine law, a view we have seen expressed in Ps 72.[11] Such a king would have to be filled "to the brim" with the divine wisdom through which he would implement *mišpat* (justice) as well as God himself would. A typical text of this vision is found in Isaiah, at the end of the "Book of Immanuel":[12]

> There shall come forth a shoot from the stump of Jesse,
>   and a branch shall grow out of his roots.
>   And the Spirit of the Lord shall rest upon him,
>   the spirit of wisdom and understanding,
>   the spirit of counsel and might,
>   the spirit of knowledge and the fear of the Lord.
> And his delight shall be in the fear of the Lord.
> He shall not judge by what his eyes see,
>   or decide by what his ears hear;
>   but with righteousness he shall judge the poor,
>   and decide with equity for the meek of the earth;
>   and he shall smite the earth with the rod of his mouth,
>   and with the breath of his lips he shall slay the wicked.

9. See vol.2, pp.195-200.
10. See Is 51:4-7; Jer 31:33; Ezek 44:24. See also vol.2, pp.195-200.
11. See ch.3 on kingly justice.
12. That is, Is 6-12; see vol.2, pp.117-129

> Righteousness shall be the girdle of his waist,
> and faithfulness the girdle of his loins.
> The wolf shall dwell with the lamb,
> and the leopard shall lie down with the kid,
> and the calf and the lion and the fatling together,
> and a little child shall lead them.
> The cow and the bear shall feed;
> their young shall lie together;
> and the lion shall eat straw like the ox.
> The suckling child shall play over the hole of the asp,
> and the weaned child shall put his hand on the adder's den.
> They shall not hurt or destroy in all my holy mountain;
> for the earth shall be full of the knowledge of the Lord
> as the waters cover the sea. (Is 11:1-9)

It is through the intermediacy of such a king that Jerusalem would attract the nations and the Lord would rule over the entire universe:

> In that day the root of Jesse shall stand as an ensign to the peoples; him shall the nations seek, and his dwellings shall be glorious. (Is 11:10)

This is the essential content of Second-Isaiah's dream for the future.[13]

Soon enough, the "universal" character of the Lord that developed in the post-exilic period,[14] together with the realization that the great majority of nascent Judaism's followers would continue to be located outside Jerusalem, paved the way for an increased interest in the "universal" medium of God's rule. The law, being tangible and thus localized, was essentially linked to the particular realm of a deity and its monarch. This is characteristic of law by its nature, whether one has in mind examples from the ancient Near East such as the Code of Hammurabi, more recent examples such as the Napoleonic Code, or our own city, state, or federal laws. Wisdom, on the other hand, cannot be localized. It is the intangible quality of every dispenser of *mišpat,* divine or human, and is naturally more likely to be perceived as universal even if it

13. See vol.2, ch.12
14. See vol.1, ch.11 and vol.2, pp.150-152.

is expressed locally by an individual ruler. That is why wisdom proved a more versatile medium for the universal deity of nascent Judaism than the law.

Wisdom and the One God

If wisdom is universal there can be no multiplicity of "wisdoms"; there must be only one. And this notion of oneness proved helpful to introduce the idea of one God to the polytheistic world in which nascent Judaism found itself. Using the terminology of wisdom rather than that of law, it was easier to speak of Yahweh, the deity of Jerusalem, as being simply *'elohim* (God).[15] The biblical reader will readily notice that whereas prophetic literature included a polemic against the deities of the nations trying to show that they are non-entities, wisdom literature did not need such polemic: it took for granted that the one wisdom reflected the oneness of God as well as of the realm he ruled, the world. The equivalence between Yahweh and God in the wisdom literature was as unequivocal as that found in the *torah* (Pentateuch), while in the *nebi'im* (Deuteronomistic History and Prophets) the polemic raged between Yahweh as God and the other deities, mainly Baal, for supremacy.

This approach proved extremely fruitful later in the Hellenistic period. Hellenism showed itself to be very aggressive in its polytheism, as in the case of Antiochus Epiphanes and the Seleucids in general.[16] But on the other hand, Hellenism was also pervaded by the tradition of wisdom—and thus universalism—that began with ancient Greek philosophy. Alexander the Great, Aristotle's pupil, played a role in developing that tradition further, and one of its later developments was Stoicism, which had an influence on both nascent Judaism and early Christianity. Dialogue between the Greeks and the Jews was possible in part because the wisdom

15. See vol.1, pp.126 and 135.
16. See vol.1, pp.153-154.

through which Yahweh created the world (Prov 3:19-20) and rules it (Job 28:21-27; Sir 8:3-4) could only be the same wisdom which the Hellenistic world itself proclaimed. It is through this language of wisdom that nascent Judaism became so successful at speaking to the world around it[17] that it could even make headway by winning large numbers of proselytes,[18] "fearers of God,"[19] and sympathizers.[20]

Personified Wisdom

hokmah (wisdom) is a feminine Hebrew noun. It is understandable then that it could be visualized as the woman of one's youth that a young man is instructed to seek after (Prov 5:15-19) and marry (Wis 8:2, 9), whereas folly is likened to the loose woman one should avoid (Prov 5:2b-14, 20, 23).[21] For this reason many commentators consider that the acrostic poem in praise of the good wife at the end of Proverbs is actually referring to wisdom and functions as an epilogue to the entire book.

The "personification" of wisdom had some practical benefits. The existential monotheism of nascent Judaism went hand in hand with an emphasis on God's utter transcendence,[22] but for God to be creator, preserver, and ruler of the world he still had to have some link to it. What was needed was a "divine representative" who would communicate between the transcendent God and his creation.[23] Being already "personified" as a woman,

17. A prime example is Philo of Alexandria.
18. See Mt 23:15 and Acts 2:10; 6:5; 13:43.
19. That is, those not yet circumcised. See Acts 10:2, 22, 35; 13:16, 26.
20. Lk 7:5
21. See also Prov 9:13-18 where the foolish woman tries to mimic "lady wisdom" (Prov 9:1-12).
22. See vol.1, pp.135-136.
23. This interest in bridging the chasm between the transcendent God and His world in this manner can be seen in the general trend in nascent Judaism to personalize God's spirit, his word *(memra)*, even his abode or presence *(shekinah)* as well as to create a complex intermediate hierarchy of angels who were assigned to peoples, nations, cities, and even individuals.

wisdom was a worthy representative of this God who, albeit universal and transcendent, was none other than Yahweh, the deity of Jerusalem,[24] himself a personal being. This was the basis behind such passages as Job 28; Prov 1:20-21; 8:1-31; 9:1-3; Wis 7:22-8:9; Sir 24:1-6, where wisdom is a divine entity. God made her before anything else (Prov 8:22-26; Wis 8:3; Sir 24:3a) in order to make her his partner in his work of creating (Prov 8:27-31; Wis 8:6; Sir 8:5-6) as well as ruling his world (Job 28:25-27; Wis 8:1, 7-8). Divine wisdom behaves as a "divine being" would: she builds her house as God would build his temple, and she invites her people to her festivities as he would (Prov 9:1-3).

The Law in the Wisdom Writings

For nascent Judaism a question naturally arose concerning the relationship between universal wisdom and the localized *torah* (Law) and *nebi'im* (Prophets) that made up its authoritative scripture. If Yahweh, the deity of Jerusalem who expressed his will specifically for Israel in his Law and through his Prophets, was in fact one and the same as the universal God who revealed his will for all humanity through his *hokmah* (wisdom), there had to be some link between the two. Nascent Judaism explained the link as general principle to specific application: intangible divine wisdom took tangible form in the written expression of the Law and its companion scripture, the Prophets. This explanation had several advantages:

1) It preserved the Law and its centrality for the nascent Jewish self-understanding. The Jew had no excuse for disobeying God's will because divine wisdom was difficult to learn. For him, this wisdom had been once and for all consigned to words in the express terms of the Law; all he had to do was follow its prescriptions.

2) It permitted dialogue with the "gentiles." They could be shown in concrete terms how far they were straying from the

24. See vol.2, p.151.

universal wisdom they sought. Sharing the Law with them and inviting them to endorse it was not so much like asking them to follow something strange and foreign but rather was an offer of help to get them back onto the right track.

3) Giving the Law a universal character helped the majority of those in the new religion of Judaism to steer away from the narrow exclusivism of some of its circles.[25] Jerusalem was after all the city of the one and only God, the God of Jews and Gentiles alike; it is the city where all nations were invited to come and share in His *mišpat* (justice) and glory.[26]

The Solomonic Literature

This explains why nascent Judaism produced wisdom literature, but why did it present Solomon as that literature's patron, the exceptionally wise king[27] who wrote many or most of the Proverbs?[28] As universal as wisdom is, it is still always actualized in particular instances and it needs to have a human source. In the period when nascent Judaism was flourishing cities formed the societal units, so in the mind of the people the natural dispenser of *mišpat* (justice) was the king. Since Judah considered the time of the united kingdom to be a golden era, either David or Solomon would have been a logical choice as the prime representative for wisdom. Why was the latter chosen over the former? Three reasons come to mind:

1) David was already established as the founder of the temple service,[29] including its psalmody.[30] Making David the patron of Wisdom literature would have given him responsibility for two very different classes of literature, so it made sense to ascribe Wisdom literature to Solomon.

25. See vol.2, pp.193-194.
26. See vol.2, ch.12.
27. Such as 1 Kg 3:4-15//2 Chr 1:3-12; 1 Kg 10:8-9.
28. See 10:1 and 25:1.
29. See vol.1, ch.15 on the Chronicler.
30. See ch.8.

2) The actual emergence of the united kingdom on the historical scene took place at its earliest only under Solomon.[31] Since a
wisdom tradition is inherent to every throne,[32] and historically
Solomon's was the throne under which this tradition most probably began, he was its logical patron.

3) An essential component of the exilic and post-exilic prophetic message is the proclamation that the Lord will have mercy
on those whom he has chastised.[33] The Deuteronomic tradition
accused Solomon of apostasy,[34] and he had been "chastised" in
that his kingdom disintegrated after his death. Since the united
kingdom under the new Jerusalem is after all a reflection of the
united kingdom that Solomon caused to be torn asunder, what
could be a greater expression of God's love and care at their fullest
except to rehabilitate also the king whose name had been black-
ened by the sin of apostasy? There was thus a certain logic in
according to Solomon a key role in exilic and post-exilic wisdom
literature: in this way he led back his apostate, exiled people now
forgiven due to their repentance, and he would again rule them,
this time according to divine wisdom.[35] He would at the same
time go beyond merely undoing the evil he once caused: the
Gentiles, who were by definition apostates in the eyes of nascent
Judaism, would be invited to seek entrance into new Jerusalem,
the city of God's fully implemented *mišpat,* through *metanoia*
(repentance) and *epistrophe pros ton theon* (return to [the only
living and true] God).[36]

---

31. See vol.1, pp.12-13.
32. Like the tribal patriarch the king was a "fatherly" figure (see ch.1).
33. See vol.2, pp.85, 139-143, 155-160, 163-185.
34. See vol.1, p.116.
35. See mainly my comments later on Ecclesiastes.
36. Acts 2;38; 3:19; 8:22; 9:35; 11:21; 17:30; 26:20; 1 Thess 1:9.

11

The Wisdom Writings

An unavoidable consequence of the universality of wisdom is that the content of the wisdom sayings in the Bible can hardly be something special or unique either to Jewish or Christian tradition or in any other such limited sense. Consider the following as but one clear example:

> Go to the ant, O sluggard;
>> consider her ways, and be wise.
>> Without having any chief,
>> officer, or ruler,
>> she prepares her food in summer,
>> and gathers her sustenance in harvest.
>> How long will you lie there, O sluggard?
>> When will you arise from your sleep?
>> A little sleep, a little slumber,
>> a little folding of the hands to rest,
>> and poverty will come upon you like a vagabond,
>> and want like an armed man. (Prov 6:6-11)

This is common to ancient Near Eastern wisdom, as are most of the sayings in the Book of Proverbs. Nevertheless, the meaning of this or any other such common saying found in the Bible is not necessarily identical in every context where it may be found. The intended meaning of any message conveyed by means of human language, regardless of length, can only be understood by taking into account its larger context. As any dictionary will readily confirm, any given word may have a wide variety of meanings and one must divine which was intended by examining the context in which the word is found. If the word is found on one page of a book, the meaning of the word is determined by the sentence, that of the sentence by the paragraph, that of the paragraph by the chapter, and that of the chapter by the entire book. Neither words nor sentences—and in the case of scripture neither verses nor even complete "sayings" or "stories"—can be understood independently. Avid book readers know that unless they have read the last word of a book, they cannot say that they have comprehended the author's entire intention and view, and the same applies to the task of understanding scripture.

It is on the premise that the canonical books are the Word of God that I read the *torah* and the *nebi'im* (the Law and the Prophets), and it is on this same premise that I shall endeavor to read the wisdom books, that is, as an integral part of the same Bible. More specifically, I shall try to demonstrate that there was an intention to establish an intimate link between the Law and wisdom by pointing out the specific means through which that goal was accomplished in the case of each wisdom book.

The Fear of The Lord

Before doing so, however, it is necessary to establish the importance of *yir'at yahweh* (the fear of the Lord) often encountered in this literature. The biblical reader will soon realize that this notion is typical of Deuteronomy and the Deuteronomistic writings and is connected with "walking in the Lord's ways" and "hearkening to the commandments" of his Law.[1] The same is true of the prophetic literature beginning with Jeremiah and contemporary with the Deuteronomic reform, and the post-exilic Chronicler's work.[2] Along with direct references to the Law, these are among the key phrases that were added to wisdom literature in order to link it to the Law and the Prophets.

---

1. Deut 4:10; 5:29; 6:2, 24; 8:6; 10:12; 13:4; 17:19; 28:58; 31:12-13; 24:14; 1 Sam 12:14, 24; 2 Kg 17:25, 28, 32, 33, 34, 36, 39, 41. In all these instances in 2 Kg 17, RSV renders the verb *yare'* (fear) with "worship".

2. Jer 32:38-40; 44:10; Zeph 3:7; Jon 1:16; Hag 1:12; 2:15; Mal 3:15; 2 Chr 19:9-10.

Proverbs

This book can be divided into sections in the following way: (a) the general title (1:1); (b) purpose of the book (1:2-7); (c) an introduction (1:8-9:18); (d) a first collection of Solomonic proverbs (10-22:16) at the end of which are attached two sets of sayings of the wise (22:17-24:22 and 24:23-34); (e) a second collection of Solomonic proverbs (25-29); (f) four appendices: the words of Agur (30:1-14), a series of numerical proverbs (30:15-33), the words of Lemuel (31:1-9), and the acrostic poem about the good wife (31:10-31).

A quick overview will show that all references to the Law or the fear of the Lord are editorial.[3] The former occurs exclusively in chs.28 and 29 at the conclusion of the entire book, just before the appendices:

Those who *forsake the law* praise the wicked,
    but those who *keep the law* strive against them. (28:4)

He who *keeps the law* is a wise son,
    but a companion of gluttons shames his father. (28:7)

If one turns away his ear from *hearing the law,*
    even his prayer is an abomination. (28:9)

Where there is no prophecy the people cast off restraint,
    but blessed is he who *keeps the law.* (29:18)

As to the fear of the Lord, already at the outset of the book, it is said to be the beginning of knowledge (1:7), and not just in a general sense but specifically the knowledge for which the proverbs of Solomon are intended (v.2a). This is clear from the verbal correspondence between vv.2a and 7 that bracket the introduction:

That men may know wisdom and instruction ...
lada'at hokmah umusar (v.2a)

---

3. They are generally considered editorial, i.e., the work of the book's final editor, because they do not fit the basic concern of the book (in this case, wisdom sayings) and yet appear at important junctures of the text so as to influence the ultimate outlook of the book itself. The aim of these editorial additions or interjections is to give the necessary twist in order to have the reader give them priority in his understanding of the book and ultimately comprehend it "in their light."

> The fear of the Lord is the beginning of knowledge;
> *yir'at yahweh rešit da'at*
> fools despise wisdom and instruction.
> *hokmah umusar 'ewilim bazu* (v.7)

Personified wisdom speaks at the beginning (1:20-33) and again at the end (8-9:6) of the introduction, and both times wisdom is equated with the fear of the Lord:

> Because they hated knowledge
> and did not choose the fear of the Lord,
> would have none of my counsel,
> and despised all my reproof,
> therefore they shall eat the fruit of their way
> and be sated with their own devices. (1:29-31)

> I, wisdom, dwell in prudence,
> and I find knowledge and discretion.
> The fear of the Lord is hatred of evil.
> Pride and arrogance and the way of evil
> and perverted speech I hate. (8:12-13)

The same idea is found at the outset of the main section of the introduction, where wisdom ("my words") is paralleled with the Law ("my commandments"):

> My son, if you receive my words
> and treasure up my commandments with you...(2:1)

Finally, in the last section of the introduction (9:7-12), just before "lady folly" is made to mimic wisdom (9:13-18), we have a reiteration of the basic principle: "The fear of the Lord is the beginning of wisdom." (v.10a)

In the second Solomonic collection, "fear of the Lord" seems to be intentionally interspersed throughout (10:27; 14:26-27; 15:16, 33; 16:6; 19:23; 22:4), as if to remind the reader that without it there could be no real wisdom. The central occurrence (15:33a)[4] reads: "The fear of the Lord is instruction in wisdom *(musar hokmah)*" (15:33a), which reprises the motto of the entire book found in 1:7. And the first and last two (10:27; 14:27;

---

4. The third out of seven and toward the middle of the collection.

19:23; 22:4) connect the fear of the Lord with life, paralleling Deuteronomy's promise of life to those who follow the precepts of the Law.

The fear of the Lord occurs one last time, and in conjunction with the promise of life, toward the middle of the first set of the "sayings of the wise," which is an attachment to the second Solomonic collection:

> Let not your heart envy sinners,
>> but continue in the fear of the Lord all the day.
>> surely there is a future,
>> and your hope will not be cut off. (23:17-18)

Ecclesiastes

This book can easily be considered the jewel of this literature. It is a good step ahead of Proverbs, yet with a subtlety absent from the later Wisdom of Sirach and Wisdom of Solomon, both of which openly equate Pentateuchal *torah* with divine wisdom. Ecclesiastes, like its predecessor Proverbs, presents itself as "The words of *qohelet, son of David, king in Jerusalem*" (1:1). Yet, unlike Proverbs which is nothing more than a collection of wisdom sayings that was transformed into an exhortation to obey the *torah* through a few references to it interspersed throughout the book, Ecclesiastes is a work that from the beginning was conceived by its author to deliver a particular message by putting to use known wisdom sayings. But what was the message?

The declared message of the book, "vanity of vanities, all is vanity" brackets the entire work (1:2 and 12:8). But why would one, if all is vanity, write a book—and, for that matter, just to declare that all is vanity? There must have been another purpose, and the author makes his intention clear right from the beginning, at least for his contemporary Jewish reader, by calling Solomon *qohelet*, to whom reference is made in the title (1:1), the start of the prologue (1:2-11), and the start of the epilogue (12:9-14), and in three other instances, near the beginning of the book (1:12), its middle (7:27) and its end (12:8). The basic clue lies in the very name *qohelet*. This noun is the feminine active participle in the *qal* form of the verb *qahal* derived from the noun *qahal*, meaning "assembly, congregation."

In biblical Hebrew verbs appear in one of seven related forms: *qal, niphal, piel, pual, hiphil, hophal,* and *hitpael*. The first six go in couples of active and passive voices, while the last usually denotes the reflexive form. Not all verbs exist in all forms. *qahal* appears only in the *niphal* form with intransitive meaning "to assemble (come together)," and the *hitpael* with transitive meaning "to assemble (bring together)." This makes out of *qohelet* (*qal* form of the verb) an exception occurring exclusively in Ecclesiastes. Moreover, instead of the masculine *qohel*, which would have been appropriate to refer to Solomon, it is the feminine *qohelet* that is used. Furthermore, at the end of the book in 12:8, we have *haqqohelet*—with the definite article—i.e., *the* assembler/congregator. Now, starting with the Deuteronomic reform, the noun *qahal* came to mean the congregation bound by the Mosaic covenant expressed in the Law, as can be gathered from its extensive use in Leviticus, Numbers, Deuteronomy, and 1 and 2 Chronicles. My conclusion is that *qohelet* is none other than the *torah* (Law), the true *hokmah* (wisdom),[5] which is the true king/ruler of Israel *in (the new) Jerusalem* (1:1, 12). The fact that *qohelet* is said to "surpass *all who were before me* in Jerusalem" (1:16; 2:7, 9) indicates the reference is to the eschatological Jerusalem. Thus, Ecclesiastes is the message to the congregation(s) of nascent Judaism confronted with Hellenism, warning them not to forget the Law. As for those who might inquire why it is that Ecclesiastes is the only book among the wisdom writings that does not have at least one passage where wisdom is personified, the answer should be clear: the entire book is an address by "lady wisdom," *qohelet*.

5. Both are feminine nouns in Hebrew.

Given this interpretation, the entire book makes sense. The thesis is that all accumulated (human) wisdom is vanity; the only real wisdom is the (divine) wisdom the Lord grants in the form of the Law. Indeed, Ecclesiastes, which seems to follow a fatalistic path, actually points to the fear of God as the way out:

> I know that whatever God does endures for ever; nothing can be added to it, nor anything taken from it; *God has made it so, in order that men should fear before him.* (3:14)

> For when dreams increase, empty words grow many: *but do you fear God.* (5:7)

> Be not righteous overmuch, and do not make yourself overwise; why should you destroy yourself? Be not wicked overmuch, neither be a fool; why should you die before your time? It is good that you should take hold of this, and from that withhold not your hand; *for he who fears God shall come forth from them all.* (7:16-18)

> Though a sinner does evil a hundred times and prolongs his life, yet I know that *it will be well with those who fear God, because they fear before him; but it will not be well with the wicked,* neither will he prolong his days like a shadow, *because he does not fear before God.* (8:12-13)

Although the noun *torah* (Law) does not occur in Ecclesiastes, the reference to it is very clear in the technical expression *šomer miswah* (one who obeys the commandment [of the Law]) in 8:5. This is corroborated by the unusually frequent use of *hatah* (to sin) and its cognates[6] since they are characteristic of and abound in the Pentateuch and the Deuteronomistic History. The interest in exhorting the reader to abide by God's will can also be seen in the author's concern with God's judgment and our accountability for our actions,[7] which means that *ultimately* all is *not quite* vanity.

That this is the intended message is confirmed by the book's ending, which to many scholars seems unexpected and out of tune with the rest of the book:

> The end of the matter; all has been heard. Fear God and keep his

6. 2:26; 5:6; 7:20, 26; 8:12; 9:2; 10:4.

7. 3:15-17; 8:5-8 (the Hebrew has *leb* [heart] for the RSV's "mind" in v.5b and *mišpat* [judgment] for RSV's "way" in v.6a); 11:9.

commandments; for this is the whole duty of man. For God will bring
every deed into judgment, with every secret thing, whether good or evil.
(12:13-14)

This conclusion can be unexpected only for one who has not
understood the rest of Ecclesiastes, because all of the main passages speaking of wisdom build toward this end. The central
theme of the book is to equate wisdom with obeying God, and
folly with disobeying God. In effect, *qohelet* argues that anything
reputed to be wisdom but which does not involve the fear of God
and observance of his commandments is in fact "vanity." Consider the following examples:

1) *qohelet's* life revolves around the quest for wisdom (1:12-
18). Ch. 2 details this quest for wisdom and ends with the
statement that God is in control, since he can grant wisdom freely,
though not to the sinner (v.26). The reader's curiosity is piqued
about how wisdom is in fact granted, but no answer is given in
chs. 3 through 6 that deal rather with the impediment to wisdom,
which is sin as announced in 2:26. This explains the use of Law
terminology in 3:14-17 and 5:6.

2) Once the incompatibility between sin and wisdom is established in the reader's mind, the second half of the book logically
concludes that wisdom flows from abiding by God's Law. Ch. 7
contains a lengthy passage on wisdom (vv.8-18) ending with "It is
good that you should take hold of this, and from that withhold
not your hand; for he who fears God shall come forth from them
all." Indeed, the seeker of wisdom will soon find that folly is
tantamount to wickedness (v.20), and wickedness is entirely the
fault of man, not God (v.29).

3) In chapter 8 *qohelet* proclaims the value of fear of the Lord in
spite of the apparent lack of divine justice: "Yet I know that it will
be well with those who fear God, because they fear before him; but
it will not be well with the wicked, neither will he prolong his days
like a shadow, because he does not fear before God." (vv.12b-13)

4) In ch. 9 *qohelet* begins by equating the righteous man with the wise man on the one hand (v.1), and evil with folly on the other (v.3), and ends by recognizing that "Wisdom is better than weapons of war; but one *sinner* destroys much good."

5) At the heart of a poem dedicated to old age (11:7-12:7) sounds the caveat "But know that for all these things God will bring you into judgment." (v.9c) In other words, it will matter after all whether you have been wise or have sinned.

6) Finally, the epilogue (12:9-14) that begins with "Besides being wise, *qohelet* also taught the people knowledge," ends with the above quoted vv.13-14 that encapsule *qohelet's* basic teaching: "Fear God and keep his commandments...For God will bring every deed into judgment ..."

Job

If the previous two books can be considered as prescriptive of how to live in accordance with Yahweh's will, the Book of Job would be descriptive of a life lived that way, as an example specifically for those subjects of the king of Jerusalem who find themselves dispersed in foreign lands. Though the reader will find no explicit mention of Jerusalem, we read at the start that Job, his siblings and friends (42:11), and his progeny until the fourth generation (1:4; 42:15-16) are all born, live, and die in the "foreign" land of Uz (1:1). The "homeland" presumed by this word "foreign" must be Jerusalem, the home of Yahweh, since we find explicit mention of Yahweh's name in the book's conclusion (42:10-17). Just as convincing is the Deuteronomic terminology found earlier in the book: Job abided by the precepts of the *torah* (1:5), "feared God" (1:9; 2:3), and when he was tested did not *sin* against God (1:8, 22; 2:3, 10).

The debate between Job and his friends, Eliphaz the Temanite, Bildad the Shuhite, and Zophar the Naamathite (chs.3-27), concludes in a deadlock and appeal is made to wisdom itself (ch.28)

that has proven inscrutable to them all, even these "wise elders,"
who are after all human:

> Man puts his hand to the flinty rock,
>> and overturns mountains by the roots.
>> He cuts out channels in the rocks,
>> and his eye sees every precious thing.
>> He binds up the streams so that they do not trickle,
>> and the thing that is hid he brings forth to light.
>> But where shall wisdom be found?
>> and where is the place of understanding?
>> Man does not know the way to it,
>> and it is not found in the land of the living.
>> The deep says, "It is not in me,"
>> and the sea says, "It is not with me."
>> It cannot be gotten for gold,
>> and silver cannot be weighed as its price.
>> It cannot be valued in the gold of Ophir,
>> in precious onyx or sapphire.
>> Gold and glass cannot equal it,
>> nor can it be exchanged for jewels of fine gold.
>> No mention shall be made of coral or of crystal;
>> the price of wisdom is above pearls.
>> The topaz of Ethiopia cannot compare with it,
>> nor can it be valued in pure gold.
>> Whence comes wisdom?
>> And where is the place of understanding?
>> It is hid from the eyes of all living,
>> and concealed from the birds of the air. (vv.9-21)

The answer lies with God himself:

> God understands the way to it,
>> and he knows its place ...
>> then he saw it and declared it;
>> he established it, and searched it out.
>> And he said to man,
>> "Behold, *the fear of the Lord, that is wisdom*;
>> and to depart from evil is understanding." (vv. 23 and 27-28)

It is then to this God that Job raises a prayer (29-31) that
concludes his words (31:40c). In it he asks to be reinstated in his

previous situation (ch.29); he defends himself (31:1-34), yet leaves it up to God to pronounce the final *judgment* (he speaks of himself here in the third person):

> Job speaks without knowledge,
>   his words are without insight.
> Would that Job were tried to the end,
> because he answers like wicked men.
> for he adds rebellion to his sin;
> he claps his hands among us,
>   and multiplies his words against God. (34:35-37)

Elihu the son of Barachel, a "youth" (32:4, 6), interrupts before God replies (38-41). The function of his speech is to prepare the reader psychologically for the divine intervention and its verdict:

1) The name Elihu means "He is my God" and that of Barachel—unique in the Old Testament—means "God blessed." The former corresponds to Job's confession in 42:1-6, while the latter points toward God's final blessing in 42:12. Also, Elihu's ire (32:2, 3, 5) reflects that of God himself (42:7).[8]

2) Elihu's speech ends on the same note as the dialogue of the elders, with a reference to divine wisdom (36:22-37:24). Ironically, a youth came to the same conclusion as the elders: if one is looking for wisdom behind events, then let one listen to the Lord.

The Lord's response boils down to the idea that God rules by his wisdom, and that wisdom is inscrutable for man. Taken within the context of the Book of Job, where the wisdom dialogue is framed by chs.1-2 and 42:7-17, this response is actually a message to the adherent of nascent Judaism for whom Job is offered as a type. Looking for the reason behind the exile is merely a cop-out: the *nebi'im* (Prophets) collection made it crystal clear that the real reason was disobedience to the Law. Now, even in a "foreign" land, what matters is still the Law: it is the wisdom sought by the people living in those foreign lands. Furthermore, the "fear of the

---

8. It is the same expression *harah 'appo* that is used in both passages.

Lord" required by the Law, not a return to and sojourn in Jerusalem, is the final guarantee for being under his aegis and benefiting from his blessings.

The Song of Songs

Ecclesiastes is also an invitation to the Gentile to recognize in the *torah* the expression of wisdom, which must lead to recognition that the universal God behind this wisdom is none other than Yahweh, the deity of Jerusalem and grantor of the Law. The same hope that Gentiles would adopt the Jewish God as their own may be found in the tradition of Second Isaiah[9] and apocalypticism,[10] according to which Jews and Gentiles would live *as one* in the eschatological Jerusalem under the rule of the one God, Yahweh. For some of the Solomonic literature, this interest in the eschatological Jerusalem eventually became paramount, and one result of the new focus is the book entitled "The Song of Songs, which is Solomon's," where an originally bridal love poem was retouched to accommodate this view.[11]

There are two clear editorial additions.[12] The first is 3:6-11, a section that speaks of Solomon's kingly procession. Here, the "king" of the original song, which is a poetic expression referring to the groom (1:4, 12; 7:5), becomes Solomon himself, specifically at his wedding (v.11). The first line of this poem, "Who is coming up from the wilderness?" corresponds to "Who is coming up from the wilderness?" (8:5a) said of the bride in the original version of the song. The intended picture with the editorial

9. See vol.2, ch.12.

10. See vol.2, pp.194-195. See also Zech 14.

11. The book's editors were probably emboldened by Ps 45 that speaks of the wedding of an Israelite or Judahite king with a Tyrian princess. Nascent Judaism will have interpreted it as referring to the marriage union between David or the Messiah with a woman from a city that was very harshly castigated in the prophetic books, beginning with Ezekiel (chs.26-28). See also Is 23; Am 1:9-10; Zech 9:2-4.

12. They can be identified as such because both are concerned with Solomon, who is not the subject matter of the rest of the book, which deals with the relation between two unnamed lovers.

changes becomes: Solomon is processing into Jerusalem and leading (1:4) his "foreign"[13] bride into his city.

The second addition consists of a set of two appendices at the end of the book (8:8-12). The first three verses tell us how the bride, representing the nations, has to detach herself from her native place, including her closest family (vv.8-9), in order to enjoy peace (v.10)—which secures order and thus life[14]—alongside her groom, i.e., in Jerusalem. The following two verses take their lead from 1:6 which mentioned the bride's vineyard she was supposed to keep in order to remain attached to her family but she decided to abandon in order to follow her groom. Here she pays her due in order to become attached to Solomon's vineyard. Moreover, this vineyard is said to be at Baal-hamon, a place whose name appears nowhere else in the Old Testament. Since the Hebrew *hamon* means "multitude," Baal-hamon would be the "baal/deity of the multitude" and could be suggestive of the multitude of the nations whose deity is said to be Baal, the nemesis of Yahweh. Thus, the intention is again to advocate the integration of the nations into the eschatological Jerusalem.

Ruth

The same concern for a "marriage" between Israel and the nations is found in the Book of Ruth. Like the bride in the Song of Solomon, the Moabite Ruth decides to leave her patrimony (2:11) and "take refuge under the wings of the Lord, the God of Israel." (2:12) She, the foreigner, was destined to become a "builder of the house of Israel" just as Rachel and Leah (4:11) and on a par with Tamar, the mother of the tribe of Judah (4:12). From her "foreign" womb would eventually be born David, the one who would some day be ruler of the eschatological Jerusalem, where Israel and the nations would live as one under Yahweh's wings.

13. She is very dark (1:5) compared to the city women who are of light complexion. This is an indication of hard work in the open sun and thus of the lower status of servants or slaves. At least she is not part of the palace constituency.

14. See ch.2.

12

Wisdom of Sirach or Ecclesiasticus

The Prologue

The final step in the direction of equating wisdom with the Pentateuchal Law was taken in the Septuagint book known as "The Wisdom of Jesus, the Son of Sirach," known also in the Latin church as Ecclesiasticus, i.e., the church book. In the prologue the "translator" explains who wrote the book and why, along with his own reasons for translating it:

> Whereas many great teachings have been given to us through the law and the prophets and the others that followed them, on account of which we should praise Israel for instruction and wisdom; and since it is necessary not only that the readers themselves should acquire understanding but also that those who love learning should be able to help the outsiders by both speaking and writing, my grandfather Jesus, after devoting himself especially to the reading of the law and the prophets and the other books of our fathers, and after acquiring considerable proficiency in them, was himself also led to write something pertaining to instruction and wisdom, in order that, by becoming conversant with this also, those who love learning should make even greater progress in living according to the law.

> You are urged therefore to read with good will and attention, and to be indulgent in cases where, despite our diligent labor in translating, we may seem to have rendered some phrases imperfectly. For what was originally expressed in Hebrew does not have exactly the same sense when translated into another language. Not only this work, but even the law itself, the prophecies, and the rest of the books differ not a little as originally expressed.

> When I came to Egypt in the thirty-eighth year of the reign of Euergetes and stayed for some time, I found opportunity for no little instruction. It seemed highly necessary that I should myself devote some pains and

labor to the translation of the following book, using in that period of time great watchfulness and skill in order to complete and publish the book for those living abroad who wished to gain learning, being prepared in character to live according to the law.

The 38th year of Ptolemy VII Euergetes is the year 132 B.C. Considering that the author of the original work in Hebrew is the translator's grandfather, and considering that "Simon the high priest, son of Onias" mentioned in 50:1 could only be the Simon II who died at the beginning of the second century, then the original author Jesus the son of Sirach (50:27) must have created this work during the 190's B.C., after Palestine came under the control of the Seleucids in 198. His intention was to emphasize the importance of the *torah* at a time when Hellenization had been threatening to undermine it, not long after Antiochus Epiphanes (175-163) provoked the Maccabean uprising.[1]

The translation was "highly necessary" in Ptolemaic Egypt of the year 132 because the issue of "instruction (in wisdom)" for a Jew in that time and place was as alive as it had been for the original writer who "was himself also led to write something pertaining to instruction and wisdom." The parallelism between the two situations, one under the Ptolemies and the other under the Seleucids, is to be found in the fact that both societies were profoundly influenced by Hellenism[2] with its stress on wisdom.[3]

What is striking about this prologue is that it ascribes to wisdom literature a place among the Hebrew scriptures, both in the grandson's and the grandfather's day.[4] "Scripture" is presented as having three parts, the first two following the established terminology of "the law and the prophets," while the description of the third part varies: "the others that followed them" (para-

1. See vol.1, pp.153-154.
2. Both these dynasties were an offshoot of Alexander the Great's empire; see vol.1, p.153.
3. See previous chapter under *Wisdom and The One God*.
4. "Whereas...Israel for instruction and wisdom...my grandfather Jesus,...instruction and wisdom." (paragraph 1)

graph 1 above), "the other books of our fathers" (paragraph 1), and "the rest of the books" (paragraph 2). This clearly indicates that the first two already formed two distinct and well rounded bodies of literature, "the first scripture" and "the second scripture" as I referred to them in vol.2.

As for Sirach itself, this prologue clearly considers it to be in the "scriptural tradition" since its basic interest is viewed as being the same as that of what the author calls "scriptures," namely, "instruction and wisdom" (paragraph 1). The latter terminology, however, does not fit "the law and the prophets," but corresponds rather to the books of Proverbs and Ecclesiastes, both of which Sirach uses profusely, besides the fact that his general purpose is the same. Two conclusions follow: (a) the wisdom tradition as expressed in Proverbs and Ecclesiastes has already taken root in nascent Judaism, and (b) its importance is such that it is considered to be on a par with "the law and the prophets," i.e., it is viewed as having "scriptural" value. This conclusion is corroborated by the remark at the end of paragraph 2 stating that these "other books" were being translated from Hebrew into Greek together with "the law and the prophets." Thus, with Proverbs and Ecclesiastes the wisdom tradition of nascent Judaism was on its way to becoming "scripture," a process that saw its culmination with Sirach.

Sirach, like Proverbs and Ecclesiastes, is intended to emphasize not only wisdom per se but more specifically the Pentateuchal *torah* as the ultimate expression of wisdom, specific rules by which one can live in order to be guided by wisdom. Both the first and third paragraphs of the prologue end on the same note:

> ... my grandfather Jesus...was himself led to write something pertaining to *instruction and wisdom,* in order that, by becoming conversant with this also, those who love learning should make even greater progress in *living according to the law.*

> ... in order to complete and publish the book for those living abroad who wished to gain *learning,* being prepared in character to *live according to the law.*

One could not possibly make clearer the belief that the ultimate goal of instruction, learning, and wisdom was to promote "living according to the law," the law clearly being the Pentateuchal *torah* in this context. Moreover, this applies not only to the Jews, but to any "lover of wisdom" from among the Gentiles since, for Sirach, the Law *is* wisdom. Indeed, the work opens with "All wisdom comes from the Lord and is with him forever" (1:1) and concludes, just before the two appended hymns in ch.51, with:

> Instruction in understanding and knowledge
> > I have written in this book,
> > Jesus the son of Sirach, son of Eleazar, of Jerusalem,
> > who out of his heart poured forth wisdom.
> > Blessed is he who concerns himself with these things,
> > and he who lays them to heart will become wise.
> > For if he does them, he will be strong for all things,
> > for the light of the Lord is his path. (50:27-29)

The Original Work

The grandson produced a work that reflected the grandfather's original intentions. Ch.1 establishes not only that *all* wisdom comes from the Lord and is with him forever, but also that this wisdom consists in the fear of him. The chapter repeats the word "wisdom" 14 times and the phrase "the fear of the Lord" 7 times, and expressly equates the two twice: "The fear of the Lord is the crown of wisdom" (v.18a), and "If you desire wisdom, keep the commandments, and the Lord will supply it for you. For the fear of the Lord is wisdom and instruction" (vv.26-27a). This last quotation introduces the triad that will become a trademark of Sirach: wisdom, law or keeping the commandments, and fear of the Lord (9:14-16; 15:1; 19:20; 21:11).

This line of thought builds to a climax in ch.24 where personified (divine) wisdom itself (vv.1-3, 9) is identified with "the book of the covenant of the Most High God, the law which Moses commanded us as an inheritance for the congregations of Jacob."

(v.23) The assertion is even made that this *torah* is itself a personal (divine) entity that creates everything and fills the creation[5] with wisdom, i.e., controls all that is:

> It [the law] fills men with wisdom, like the Pishon,
> and like the Tigris at the time of the first fruits.
> It makes them full of understanding, like the Euphrates,
> and like the Jordan at harvest time.
> It makes instruction shine forth like light,
> like the Gihon at the time of vintage.
> Just as the first man did not know her perfectly,
> the last one has not fathomed her;
> for her thought is more abundant than the sea,
> and her counsel deeper than the great abyss. (vv.25-29)

That this is the very center of Sirach's teaching is reflected in the fact that precisely at this juncture the original author, Jesus son of Sirach, interjects his own voice into the text to state the purpose of the work:

> I went forth like a canal from a river
> and like a water channel into a garden.
> I said, "I will water my orchard
> and drench my garden plot";
> and lo, my canal became a river,
> and my river became a sea.
> I will again make instruction shine forth like the dawn,
> and I will make it shine afar;
> I will again pour out teaching like prophecy,
> and leave it to all future generations.
> Observe that I have not labored for myself alone,
> but for all who seek instruction. (vv.30-34)

Sirach as Scripture

It is immediately apparent that the author's intention here is nothing less than putting his own wisdom teaching—and with it that of Proverbs and Ecclesiastes—on a par with prophecy as a

---

5. The reference to paradise and its four rivers is an unmistakable reference to the Genesis creation story.

work worth preserving for future generations (v.32; also v.34b). In other words, he is attributing "scriptural" status to these works, and this is not the only way he tries to get this message across. Toward the end of the book's first part composed mainly of clusters of proverbs (1-42:14), we have a lengthy passage devoted to the scribe who seeks wisdom (compare 38:24 and 39:1):

> On the other hand he who devotes himself
> to the study of the law of the Most High
> will seek out the wisdom of all the ancients,
> and will be concerned with prophecies;
> he will preserve the discourse of notable men
> and penetrate the subtleties of parables;
> he will seek out the hidden meanings of proverbs
> and be at home with the obscurities of parables.
> He will serve among great men and appear before rulers;
> he will travel through the lands of foreign nations,
> for he tests the good and the evil among men.
> He will set his heart to rise early
> to seek the Lord who made him,
> and will make supplication before the Most High;
> he will open his mouth in prayer
> and make supplication for his sins.
> If the great Lord is willing,
> he will be filled with the spirit of understanding;
> he will pour forth words of wisdom
> and give thanks to the Lord in prayer.
> He will direct his counsel and knowledge aright,
> and meditate on his secrets.
> He will reveal instruction in his teaching,
> and will glory in the law of the Lord's covenant.
> Many will praise his understanding,
> and it will never be blotted out;
> his memory will not disappear,
> and his name will live through all generations.
> Nations will declare his wisdom,
> and all the congregation will proclaim his praise;
> if he lives long, he will leave a name greater than a thousand,
> and if he goes to rest, it is enough for him.

> I have yet more to say, which I have thought upon,
> and I am filled, like the moon at the full. (39:1-12)

The final verse shifts to the first person, which shows that in what precedes it the author has presented a portrait of himself. Moreover, the passage's importance is reflected by its location near a major turning point in the book, the transition from the first part (1-42:14) to the second part (42:15-50:29). This passage is not right at the boundary but it clearly looks forward to the second part, as can be seen in the reference "the works of the Lord" in 39:16a, since that is precisely the topic Sirach turns to at the start of the second part where we again hear the author's own voice: "I will now call to mind the works of the Lord, and will declare what I have seen." Therefore, with links to both the first and last parts, this passage (39:1-12) functions as a hinge between the two and is uniquely important for understanding Sirach. A closer look at its content will reveal the following:

1) "The law of the Most High," "the wisdom of all the ancients," and "the prophecies" correspond to the tripartite scriptures.

2) The specific field of this book itself, however, is wisdom, as is evident from vv.2-7, describing the necessary preliminary study, and v.8a that refers to the writing of the book.

3) Wisdom is inseparable from the Law. In the midst of a series of clauses proclaiming how the wise scribe will commit his wisdom to words and will teach others, we hear that "he will glory in the law of the Lord's covenant" (v.8b)

4) The wise scribe's words will "never be blotted out" (v. 9), i.e., they will become scripture, an integral part of the heritage of "all the congregation." And not only his words, but his very name "will live through all generations" because he himself will become a scriptural figure (v.10 parallels 44:15, which discusses other scriptural figures).

Wisdom and Scripture

The centrality of the Law, and by extension of the entire tripartite scripture, becomes even clearer in the book's second part. Here the author begins by speaking of the works of the Lord (42:15) which the wise man is supposed to do (39:1-12, 16a). What are the "works of the Lord"? First and foremost, this phrase reflects the author's premise that universal wisdom tradition must be based on the understanding that everything that exists is ultimately the Lord's—i.e., the biblical God's—creation:[6]

> I [the wise scribe] will now call to mind the works of the Lord,
>> and will declare what I have seen.
>> By the words of the Lord his works are done ...
>> He has ordained the splendors of his wisdom,
>> and he is from everlasting to everlasting.
>> Nothing can be added or taken away,
>> and he needs no one to be his counselor. (42:15 and 21)

It is with this premise in mind, which is none other than that of the Pentateuchal Law (Gen 1-3), that Sirach's "story of (divine/eternal) wisdom" slides from the domain of nature/creation to that of human history, again following the pattern of the Book of Genesis. Indeed, after having concluded his recounting of the Lord's "creative" activity with the words: "Many things greater than these lie hidden, for we have seen but few of his works. For the Lord has made all things, and to the godly he has granted wisdom," (43:32-33) he immediately begins the following section with: "Let us now praise famous men, and our fathers in their generations." (44:1) Furthermore, the intimate connection between "natural history" and "human history" can be seen in his view that both actually are the reflection of God's glory (compare 42:16-17, 25 with 44:2-3).[7]

On the other hand, Sirach's "human history" itself is none other than the "scriptural" story preserved in "the law and the

6. See ch.2.

7. See also 44:7, 13, 19; 45:2-3, 20, 23, 26.

prophets" until Nehemiah (49:13). The mention of the latter, incidentally, is another indication that the *ketubim* (Writings) collection, of which Proverbs and Ecclesiastes are a part, was already on its way to being "scripturalized." The books of Ezra and Nehemiah are the only pre-Sirach works that mention Nehemiah, so one or both must have been his source for this reference—and they are in fact counted among the *ketubim* in the Hebrew canon of the Old Testament, located right at the end just before the two Books of Chronicles. The entire story "of the famous men, our fathers" (44:1) is recapitulated in 49:14-16, which is a clear indication that the story embedded in the tripartite scriptures was, in Sirach's view, the scene in which (divine/eternal) wisdom came to be revealed.

Wisdom Literature as Scripture

Before the book's second section concludes with a call to "bless the God of all, who in every way does great things" (50:22a),[8] the "scriptural" story revealing wisdom is augmented by the witness of High Priest Simon II, a contemporary of the author himself who is thus including his own times in the "scriptural" story. This can only be a sign of Sirach's conviction that Simon's witness *as rendered in 50:1-21* is an integral part of "scripture" and that consequently the entire Book of Sirach—and with it the entire wisdom tradition whose heir he is—is an integral part of the scriptural tradition of nascent Judaism.

The reader of the passage on Simon cannot escape the feeling that the interest in him is specifically due to his role *as high priest.* Furthermore, the priests around him are called the "sons of Aaron" (vv.13 and 16), which may be related to the greater interest expressed earlier in Aaron compared to Moses himself (17 verses [45:6-22] as compared to only 5 [45:1-5]). The interest in Aaron's progeny through Phinehas (45:23-26) may also reflect the focus on Aaron's priesthood. Taken together, all of this sounds

---

8. Compare with 42:15. The conclusion of the entire book appears in 50:27-29.

very similar to the post-exilic priestly tradition, from which the Pentateuch in its present form was developed, and which especially formed the content of its large central section comprising Exodus 19 through Numbers 25.[9]

On the other hand, in the Old Testament literature the expression "the sons of Aaron" occurs most frequently in the 2 volumes of Chronicles, outside the priestly section of the Pentateuch. There may be a direct link between the Chronicles and Sirach,[10] and the unexpected mention of the "singers"[11] in 50:18 may be evidence of this. Corroborating that view is their mention earlier (47:9) in a passage speaking of what David did for the temple (47:8-10), more than just a passing mention since it takes one verse out of these three and one out of a total of eleven devoted to David. When all this is taken together with the inclusion of Nehemiah as the last figure in the "scriptural" story (49:13), it tells us of the effort Sirach is putting into ensuring the *ketubim* are honored as highly as the Pentateuch, the "first scripture." In other words, these writings were not yet universally considered to be the "third scripture," and he was arguing that they should be so honored.

Wisdom of Solomon

A Greek-language offshoot of Ecclesiasticus, but with a rather polemical tone, is found in the Septuagint (there is no original Hebrew version). Though the title "Wisdom of Solomon" clearly suggests this belongs with the wisdom literature, the first part (chs.1-5) actually uses the terminology of "righteous versus wicked" more characteristic of apocalyptic literature. The second part (chs.6-9) portrays Solomon in search of wisdom, at the end

9. See vol.1, chs.13 and 14.

10. See vol.1, ch.15.

11. Singers and their position in the temple service are of a special concern only in 1 Chr. 15-16. See vol.1, p.149.

of which he prays to the "God of my fathers" to grant it to him (ch.9). Through wisdom, we hear, men were "saved" (v.18)—another apocalyptic commonplace.[12] This introduces part three (chs.10-19) which reviews the biblical account from the beginning of Genesis up to the event of exodus—the event of salvation par excellence—presented as the work of wisdom.

The heavy concentration on the exodus from Egypt (10:15-19:22) combined with the apocalyptic terminology suggests the book is addressed to Alexandrian Jews. The author is worried about their being swayed by the Hellenistic views extant in Alexandria, the cultural capital of the Hellenistic world during the first century B.C. Thus, Solomon, as holder of true wisdom, addresses himself to "the rulers of the earth" (1:1) and "kings and judges of the ends of the earth" (6:1), reminding them that "wisdom will not enter a deceitful soul, nor dwell in a body enslaved to sin" (1:4) and that they will be judged by the God who granted wisdom to him according to whether they have kept the Law:

> For your dominion was given you from the Lord,
> and your sovereignty from the Most High,
> who will search out your works and inquire into your plans.
> because as servants of his kingdom you did not rule rightly,
> nor keep the law,
> nor walk according to the purpose of God,
> he will come upon you terribly and swiftly,
> because severe judgment falls on those in high places. (6:3-5)

The author's concern to draw his Alexandrian fellows away from Hellenistic wisdom teachings and toward strict obedience to the wisdom embedded in the *torah* can be clearly seen in perhaps the most interesting and valuable feature of this book: the author's profuse use of current Hellenistic philosophical terminology to speak of this wisdom connected with the biblical God:

> For in her there is a spirit that is intelligent, holy,
> unique, manifold, subtle,

12. See vol. 2, pp. 209 and 211.

mobile, clear, unpolluted,
distinct, invulnerable, loving the good, keen,
irresistible, beneficent, humane,
steadfast, sure, free from anxiety,
all-powerful, overseeing all,
and penetrating through all spirits
that are intelligent and pure and most subtle.
For wisdom is more mobile than any motion;
because of her pureness she pervades and penetrates all things.
For she is a breath of the power of God,
and a pure emanation of the glory of the Almighty;
therefore nothing defiled gains entrance into her.
For she is a reflection of eternal light,
a spotless mirror of the working of God,
and an image of his goodness.
Though she is but one, she can do all things,
and while remaining in herself, she renews all things. (7:22-27a)

Though here we find the philosophical terms of the times, this perfect wisdom[13] is also described with terms typical of the biblical God. In every generation it "passes into holy souls and makes them friends of God and prophets" (v.27b), and it is paralleled with God's own "holy spirit" (9:17). The latter may be a reference to Isaiah 11, where we are told of a universal ruler and judge[14] filled with the wisdom bestowed by the spirit of the Lord in a passage that also uses exodus terminology (vv.15-16) and speaks of the "gathering of the dispersed" (vv.11-14) in reference to Alexandrian Jews.

The movement to dialogue with Hellenistic wisdom which began in Proverbs found an interesting expression in this vesting of the Law with the garb of Hellenistic wisdom. This step will later prove momentous for Paul's apostolic preaching, as well as for the christology of Colossians, Ephesians, the Gospel of John, and Hebrews. It will also prove helpful to the church Fathers who

---

13. There are 21 epithets for wisdom in this passage, a number which may be intentional: 3 times 7, the latter being the number expressing divine perfection (see Rev 1:4, 7, 13, 16; 3:1; 4:5; 5:6).

14. Compare with Wis 1:1 and 6:1.

took upon themselves the furtherance of dialogue with Greeks while trying to remain faithful to the New Testament gospel originally expressed in Judaic terms.

13

The Function of Wisdom Literature

The "third scripture" is, or at least should be, a "thorn in the flesh" of Christendom, especially as it developed in Western Europe and North America. The increasing stress on the biblical notion of "chosenness," coupled with the "Greek versus barbarian" terminology and the understanding that the Roman empire was its own self-sufficient universe eventually produced the monstrous notion of *natio Christiana* (the Christian "nation") during the Middle Ages—and European Christendom came to perceive itself as a universal norm. Hence the Crusades; the pogroms against Jew, Muslim, and any kind of "infidel"; the Inquisition; the intolerance of contemporary fundamentalists toward anyone who does not share their views; and the end-of-the-world timetables set by so many Christians of all kinds warning that their savior is going to take care of them and damn those who disagree with them.

Wisdom literature tempers the idea of "chosenness" that gave rise to such terrible consequences, by reminding us that others are as much God's creation as we are. Our own chosenness consists in the fact that we shall be held accountable for living our lives according to every iota of the *entire* scripture: first, second, third, and also the fourth (the New Testament). This is why the liturgical life of both Judaism and Christianity is structured around readings of scripture. The readings in the synagogues of nascent Judaism were three: one from the Law, another from the Prophets, and the third from the Writings. The early church added readings from the New Testament. The readings in our own services also follow a certain order: first the Old Testament, then the "Apostle," and finally the "Gospel." This means that one is to follow a path that culminates with Jesus Christ himself. However, it does not mean that once the level of the Gospels is attained, the Christian may forego the "Apostle" and the Old Testament: they are all, and all together, the *one* Word of God.[1] Within the realm of the Old Testament itself, there is a gradation from the Writings, to the Prophets, and then to the Law. This is still witnessed to by the church's liturgical calendar, which stipulates that the Writings are to be read more frequently during Great Lent, because that is considered a period for instruction of catechumens, culminating in baptism at Easter. It is, by the way, an indication that wisdom literature was part of the larger corpus referred to as *anaginoskomena,* i.e., "things to be read," or "good for reading," and thus edifying material. Edifying in which sense? As an introduction to the Law that it introduces as the true wisdom for wisdom seekers. The Prophets, the second step in this introduction to the Law as the expression of God's will, warn us of the danger of utter destruction *by God himself* of whoever does not keep that Law.

We contemporary Christians living in the "West," who virtually control the fate of our planet, have largely forgotten that the *ketubim* (Writings), which include mainly the wisdom books, are an integral part of our Bible. As a result our viewpoint is often an "unbiblical," individually-based outlook on what "life" is all about. But if we would only take seriously the wisdom of the Biblical wisdom literature, our world—the good world created by the wisdom of the God of the *torah* (Law) and the *nebi'im* (Prophets)—would become itself and in itself a foretaste of what God's rule and kingdom are and will be. In that case the real challenge will be to realize that it is we ourselves, not the "outsiders," who must change. After all, it is to *us,* not the "outsiders," that *our* Lord is saying:

> You have heard that it was said, "You shall love your neighbor and hate your enemy." But I say to you, Love your enemies and pray for those

1. See further on this matter my chapter on the authority of the Old Testament.

who persecute you, so that you may be sons of your Father who is in heaven; for he makes his sun rise on the evil and on the good, and sends rain on the just and the unjust. For if you love those who love you, what reward have you? Do not even the tax collectors do the same? And if you salute only your brethren, what more are you doing than others? Do not even the Gentiles do the same? You, therefore, must be perfect, as your heavenly Father is perfect. (Mt 5:43-48)

If the texts appropriate for catechumens are first and foremost the wisdom writings, how much more appropriate are they for those who are neither Christians nor even catechumens? With such people the language of wisdom is our *sole* bridge of communication and must remain so until they have acknowledged that true wisdom lies in the Law of the Lord. Only then are we allowed to begin using the language of the *torah* and the *nebi'im*. Too often we do the opposite: we condemn "outsiders" on the basis of the latter texts while we do not bother applying even one iota of the *ketubim* to ourselves—assuming we even bother to read them! Unless we Christians give heed to the teachings of the wisdom writings, we are bound to find a rude awakening in God's kingdom which is as much communal as the world is, since both are God's. If we did take heed, we would find that we have more cause to condemn ourselves rather than the outsiders, whom we would come to see as members with us of God's community.

III

The Old Testament in the Church

14

Continuity and Discontinuity Between the Old Testament and the New Testament

The three volumes of this series have now surveyed the entire body of scriptures that came to be known as the Old Testament, and it is time to address some issues pertaining to that body as a whole. First and foremost is the matter of the relationship between the Old Testament and the New Testament. In what sense are these two separate collections of scriptural books really one single book of scriptures? This has been a perennial issue in the history of Christian thought and has given rise to numerous individual controversies, each different from its predecessors though revolving around the same subject. Each time someone would approach the subject from a new and different perspective; each time someone would ask new questions requiring a new answer. However, in all the debate there was always one common premise shared by all and questioned by none: everyone accepted the unity of the Bible as the one book of the Church.

Until this century the only significant exception dates back 1800 years to Marcion, whose belief in two gods necessarily entailed an essential difference between two sets of scriptures. The church's response to Marcion is well known and in fact set the tone for all subsequent debate—for afterwards, until today, no one dared to question the fundamental premise that the Bible is inherently one book.

The Contemporary Debate

But what of the contemporary debate? Can it still be viewed as another post-Marcionite discussion, another variation on the same old tune of the one-Bible premise? Or is it comparable in both nature and consequence to the one sparked by Marcion himself? I believe the latter to be true. Consider the effect of some key changes in terminology that have come about in this century. With the experience of the Jewish holocaust during World War II and the founding of the Israeli state in 1948, a large and theologically influential sector within European and then American Protestantism, and later even Catholicism, officially endorsed the terminology of "Hebrew Scriptures" when referring to the Old Testament writings.[1] Obviously this does not refer merely to the language of these scriptures; otherwise one would expect to hear the term "Greek Scriptures,"[2] employed in reference to the New Testament. Instead, we encounter only such expressions as "New Testament" or "Greek New Testament," or "Christian Scriptures." Such terminology clearly implies a split within the body of scriptures that two thousand years of Christian tradition has recognized as one book. In other words, we are not faced here with a simple change of perspective concerning a minor issue; rather, we are dealing with a radically new position that negates a longstanding, well-established Christian premise.

1. My reader's attention is kindly drawn to the fact that I am not debating here the use of this expression by non-Christian Jews. Their use of it is accurate and logical both formally and materially: formally, because their scriptures are in Hebrew; and materially, because this body of scriptures is their Holy Writ. Even then, from a general standpoint, a more neutral and matter-of-fact reference to the Old Testament would be "Jewish scriptures" (in the sense of "the scripture of Judaism"), as long as both Old and New Testaments are referred to as "Christian scriptures" (in the sense of "the scripture of Christianity")—just as the *Qur'an* is "the scripture of Islam"—given that within one religion or belief there can be only *one indivisible* set of scriptures (see on this matter further below).

2. Even if this term is found occasionally, it is at best ambiguous and at worst inaccurate, since it could mean "The Scriptures of the Greeks," which is incorrect. And if the intended meaning is the "Greek Scriptures of the church," why is it that one never finds the expression "Hebrew Scriptures of the church"?

The consequences of this new theological stand are not trivial. It inevitably leads to the abandonment of several other premises essential to the Christian tradition, to the extent that we must ask ourselves whether we are not actually confronted with a heresy. I mean by this term its original sense of separation or parting of the ways, the choice of a different path that is not just a different expression of the same way but is rather an essentially different and separate way, one which leads to a different destination. Specifically, those who endorse this new approach to the Bible depart from the Christian tradition in three important ways:

1) One consequence of dividing the Bible into two books is the belief that each book is really addressed to a different community. The "Hebrew Scriptures" are addressed to Israel, equated simply and exclusively with the contemporary Jews, whereas the New Testament is addressed to the church. The two are completely separate and cannot be combined at all; after all, Israel—i.e., the Jews—is both a national and a theological entity, whereas the church is only a theological one. Consequently, it is only the Jews that the Hebrew Scriptures are concerned with, and the church should read them accordingly, i.e., as dealing with a second party which is not itself.[3] Some adherents of this position take the separation between Israel and the church to such an extreme that they say the term Israel always refers exclusively to the non-Christian Jews even in the New Testament.

2) The corollary to the preceding point is that God now has two "communities." Until the advent of Jesus Christ, God implemented His *oikonomia* (plan for salvation) for mankind through Israel, i.e., the Jews. But then beginning with Jesus Christ this one God of both sets of scriptures started to manage his one *oikonomia* via two separate channels, Israel and the church; i.e., via two separate covenants, the one not annulling the other. This scheme actually makes the church's

---

3. In order not to misrepresent the holders of such a view, I should add that although the "Hebrew Scriptures" are said to be exclusively concerned (i.e., dealing) with the Jews, they nevertheless concern the church since they speak of the God of the church.

covenant subservient to Israel's in that the Christian ministry consists in little more than pointing out to the world (the Gentiles) that through the Jews God is implementing the salvation of all even now. Put otherwise, the church's calling consists of being a minister to the Jews or an interpreter of their meaning to the rest of humanity, since it is through this ongoing experience of the Jews that God is unfolding his ultimate plan for mankind. Theologically speaking, Christians are essentially the apostles of the "mystery of Israel" (Rom 11:25-32) to the world at large.

3) Some theologians push the matter even further. They say that in the strictest sense it is the "Hebrew Scriptures" that are the sole *graphe* (scripture), Word of God. The New Testament writings represent only a particular interpretation of this *graphe,* just as the post-70 A.D. rabbinical traditions reflect a different exegesis of the same *graphe.* Thus, not only is the church's mission subservient to that of the Jews, but also the New Testament, latter part of the Holy Writ of the church, is only secondary in authority when compared to the "Hebrew Scriptures." In other words, a true interpretation of the New Testament should not consist of a mere effort at a more truthful understanding of its teaching; it must also entail a correction of those teachings wherever they are allegedly contrary to the "Hebrew Scriptures." An extreme example of such an approach can be seen in the assertion that anti-Israel statements in the "Hebrew Scriptures" express well-deserved divine indictments, whereas the slightest criticism of Jews in the New Testament reflects inexcusable anti-Semitism on the part of a misled or hateful human author.

Similarity between the Marcionite and Contemporary Approaches

The similarity between the Marcionite stand and the one I have just described is crystal clear. Marcion utterly separated the two parts of the one Bible by advocating a scripturally unwarranted duality in the one God referred to throughout the Bible. The modern approach does the same thing but in a more ingeniously subtle way. It introduces a duality within the one community covenanted by the one God, the corollary being the introduction of a duality in God's *oikonomia* and therefore in the covenant itself. You might say that while Marcion introduced the duality on the *theological* level, his modern counterparts have established it on the *"oikonomical"* level. Be that as it may, one thing is sure: in either case, the one Christian Bible is split into two separate entities. The question is then: Is such a division warranted?

The answer to this question must not proceed from an extra-biblical premise. That was Marcion's Achilles' heel: he started with the gnostic assumption of the two gods and proceeded to read it into the Bible. In order to discredit him, Irenaeus needed only to point out that the New Testament itself witnessed to its belief in the God of the Old Testament as himself the God and Father of Jesus Christ. A similar fate awaits anyone else who appeals to a post-biblical starting point, be it Christian tradition or post-70 A.D. Jewish tradition. Anything post-biblical is, after all ipso facto extra-biblical. On the other hand, considering the nature of the question we are asking now, starting with the premise of the one Bible is not helpful either. It is this premise itself—at least in its classical Christian form—which is under examination. So we must begin our investigation by examining an antecedent premise: in what sense, if any, is each of these two sets of scriptures itself a unity? Only after we have answered that question will we be able to establish if and in what sense they should be viewed separately as two or together as one.

The Oneness of the Old Testament

I credit James Barr with instituting the healthy moratorium that has been put on the so-called "biblical theologies,"[4] but I believe

4. J. Barr, *Semantics of Biblical Language,* 1961.

such endeavors were doomed from the beginning. At first they began with the assumption of the oneness of a given set of scriptures and then tried at best to find, or at worst to express a preference for, the most suitable theological notion that would hold them together, such as exodus, *torah,* covenant, election, salvation, Kingdom of God, and the like. Once they settled on their chosen theme, they would proceed to read the scriptures from that particular perspective. Later the mood swung away from harmonizing different views within a set of scriptures to emphasizing the diverse, even dissimilar, "theologies" of the various biblical authors. The new breed of biblical theologian then acknowledged the Old and New Testaments as "*sets*" of scriptures only formally, as a convenient method of grouping them together when writing books about them. Now, at first glance these two approaches to writing "biblical theologies" seem to be opposites, but in reality they begin with the same premise. Both view the Old Testament as scriptures which witness to the revelation or actions of a God whose oneness and uniqueness, let alone existence, are assumed to be self-evident. But upon closer scrutiny, this very idea that there can only be one God, an idea which is taken for granted in any of these treatments of the Old Testament, proves to be itself an extra-biblical assumption. Indeed, its provenance can be traced to the Christianized Roman Empire and especially to the beginning of the second millennium when scholastic theology in Western Europe fully integrated the philosophical approach into its presentation of the Christian faith. By and large then, the "biblical theologies" did little more than force the Old Testament to conform to a procrustean bed of their authors' own imagination.

If we abandon this post-biblical and therefore extra-biblical approach to the bible, what do we find? A radical difference between the texture of our own mental world and that of the biblical text. Whereas we perceive the oneness of God as a universally valid premise, in the Old Testament it is a premise exclusively for the biblical authors, or at most not necessarily endorsed by their contemporaries. The oneness of God in the Old Testament is not a self-evident premise, but rather a proposition which the biblical reader is exhorted to endorse as a premise in order to understand what the text is trying to say concerning this God. In other words, whereas our mental syntax says, "The self-evident one universal deity is the God spoken of in the Bible," the biblical mental syntax says, "The biblical God is (to be assumed as) the one universal deity."

As it stands in its final canonical form the Old Testament no doubt reflects the belief in one universal God who is none other than the biblical God himself. However, it is no less true that, as it stands, the Old Testament bears the imprimatur of post-exilic nascent Judaism whose God was conceived as the one universal deity. The priestly theologians of nascent Judaism reinterpreted the pre-exilic and exilic formative traditions from their own point of view, whose basic tenet was the oneness of God. What most modern theologians de facto fail to take into account is the fact that those formative traditions arose within a polytheistic environment endorsed by the Israelite and Judahite authors themselves as part of their worldview.

It is this drastic post-exilic reinterpretation of older traditions that lies at the heart of Old Testament literature and holds it together as one book. Indeed, the covenants are multiple: the Noachic, the Abrahamic, the Mosaic-Sinaitic, the Davidic, the new covenant (Jer 31:31-34), the *'ebed yahweh* covenant (Is 42:6; 49:8), the post-exilic covenant of peace (Ezek 34:25; 37:26; Is 54:10); the new Jerusalem covenant (54:10; 55:3; 59:21; 61:8).[5] Even the so-called unique event of exodus is multiple: compare Ezek 20:41 with vv. 9-10 and 14, and v. 42 with vv. 5-6 and especially Ex 6:8. The elections are multiple: Ephraim/Joseph and

5. It is immaterial for our argument whether the last four refer to one and the same covenant or not.

then Judah (Ps 78:56-72; see also 1 Sam 13:13-14; 16:11-13), and so are the rejections (Jer 7:12-15; 26:6). And no wonder, since this is only a corollary to the fact that there were two historically independent kingdoms in whom Yahweh was honored as a deity: Israel/Ephraim and Judah (2 Sam 5:1-4: Is 7:1-9; Jer 3:6-13; 23:24; Ezek 23; 35:10). In fact, these never became one entity except in exilic and post-exilic theological wishful thinking (Jer 31:31; Ezek 37:15-28).[6] The inescapable conclusion: it is the post-exilic Judaic premise of the oneness of God that forced a certain aspect of oneness and uniqueness to the biblical notions of election, exodus, covenant, and even the one Israel, which are all—including the last one—ultimately theological notions or entities.

The Judaic Scripture

This conclusion is corroborated by Judaism's approach to the Old Testament. The traditional designation for that canonical literature can be either the singular *he graphe* (scripture) or the plural *hai graphai* (the scriptures). The plural obviously refers to the entirety of the writings, and its use shows that the historical fact of multiple human authorship is acknowledged. This recognition is also reflected in the traditional numbering of 24 books and the traditional naming of those books according to their reputed authors, e.g., the five books of Moses, the Psalms of David, Isaiah, Jeremiah, Ezekiel, etc.[7]

The singular *graphe*, on the other hand, can mean a particular quotation (e.g., Mk 12:10; Lk 4:21; Jn 13:18; Acts 8:35) or scripture in its entirety, i.e., the Old Testament as a whole.[8] This latter

6. See vol.2, pp.157-158.

7. Just to name one classic example, in his letters to the Romans, Paul refers to Hosea (9:25), Isaiah (9:27, 20; 10:16, 20, 21), Moses (10:5, 19), and David (11:9) as authors of the different passages taken from the books traditionally attributed to them.

8. See especially Acts 8:35 cited above, where "this scripture [*tes graphes tautes*]" refers back to the scriptural quotation of vv. 32b-33 which was introduced as "a passage of scripture [*perioche tes graphes*]" in v. 32a.

usage is interesting insofar as it exhibits a perception of the canonical scriptures as a unity, not just as individual writings. And the reason for that perception is an even more basic belief in the unity of God himself. In fact, for the Judaic mind it is God who unites the different scriptures into one because he is ultimately the one author of them all. This can be clearly seen from the following:

1) *he graphe* is commonly used as the subject of verbs such as *legein* (say, Jn 7:38, 42; Rom 4:3; 10:11), *proidein* (foresee, Gal 3:8), and *synkleisai* (shut in, Gal 3:22), which obviously denotes a certain personification of scripture. The contexts of the last two instances clearly show that the logical subject is none other than God.[9] The interchangeability between "God" and "scripture" can be seen at its clearest in Rom 9:17 where Paul writes: "For scripture says to Pharaoh, 'I have raised you up for the very purpose of showing my power in you, so that my name may be proclaimed in all the earth.'"

2) Besides his oneness, another corollary of God's universality was his transcendence, which in turn required the use of intermediaries between him and his created world. Among those intermediaries was the *torah*. Indeed, in nascent Judaism this term did not refer only to the Pentateuch, but also to the instructions delivered at Sinai contained therein and even their personification as pre-existent *torah*. The importance of this hypostasized *torah* can be seen in the rabbinic teaching that the world itself was created for her sake, i.e., for the sake of her implementation and thus in order to witness to her. This view of the Pentateuchal *torah* came to be applied to the entirety of scripture to the extent that a quasi-independent entity called "scripture" was seen to be expressing itself through the biblical text of the Old Testament. Twice Paul asks the rhetorical question, "What does scripture say?" Once he answers with words spoken by Sarah (Gen 21:10 in Gal 4:30) and once with words spoken by the biblical author (Gen 15:6 in Rom 4:3).

---

9. See also Gal 3:16 where *legein* occurs without any subject at all.

While God's oneness was axiomatic for nascent Judaism, the only historical matrix for the post-exilic community was the pre-exilic kingdoms of Israel and Judah, each with its own unique traditions. It was both natural and necessary then for Judaism to read back into that pre-exilic period its own understanding of the one, transcendent, and universal God. Hence the full equation between the universal God and the originally local deity Yahweh in the reworking of the traditions pertaining to those two kingdoms. As evidence that this is really what happened, suffice it to mention here the multiplicity of the patriarchal deities in Genesis on the one hand, and, on the other, the perennial struggle between Yahweh and Baalism in Israel and Judah as witnessed in Deuteronomy, the Deuteronomistic History, and the prophetic literature.

A closer look at the writings covering the pre-exilic period—i.e., the Pentateuch, the Deuteronomistic History, the two books of Chronicles, and the pre-exilic prophetic sayings, as well as the "historical psalms" (Ps 78, 105, 106, 135, 136)—reveals that this period is presented as one continuous history. However, God is the primary agent of this history as well as its subject;[10] the role of human beings always seems to be reduced to a negative one; that is, they are always opposing or trying to undo God's work! Consequently, not only is the Old Testament held together as a unity essentially by the notion of the oneness of God, but also a critical approach to the text reveals that its central concern is what may be called the "history of God," or more accurately the "story of God"—rather than the "story of Israel." Indeed, the biblical notion of Israel with its essentially positive overtones is itself another theological product of nascent Judaism. From the Old Testament perspective, Israel (viewed either as Abraham's offspring or as shaped at exodus) is not the self-defining subject of the story but literally an outcome of God's "historical" activity,

10. Older scholarship liked to speak of the Bible as the book of the "acts of God."

created and defined by God who preceded it and rules over it as his own creation.

But if the texture of the Old Testament is essentially that of a "story" of the biblical God, one is faced with a series of questions. Is the notion of history compatible with a God who is one, universal, and transcendent? Why did Judaism want to—or why did it have to—link the pre-exilic Israelite and Judahite local deity known as Yahweh with the post-exilic Judaic universal God? What was the nature of that linkage? The way to an answer is illuminated by the axiom *ex nihilo nihil* ("out of nothing comes nothing"). The very idea of a deity, as any other idea, is always "bound" in the human mind, that is, it depends on a substratum or point of reference in order to be conceived. And in the ancient Near East, which was the immediate environment of the Old Testament literature, the point of reference for the idea of deity was essentially the idea of kingship. The king, while being localized, at the same time ruled over an extended domain, both aspects of his existence being necessary for him to be considered a king. The tangible, confined royal throne was itself the expression of royal rule over the entire *'eres* (land/earth/universe) lying in his royal domain. So was the case with the deity—any deity. From its heavenly throne, usually the top of a mountain, reflected in its earthly throne, usually the inner sanctuary of the temple in the capital city, the deity ruled sovereignly over its "world." Thus, divine universality did not exclude divine particularity—in fact, it *necessarily* entailed localism and particularism. It is no wonder then that the ultimate universalism of Ezekiel, Second Isaiah, Third Isaiah, and Second Zechariah included, without the slightest difficulty or need for explanation, the localism of the new temple and the new Jerusalem.

If this is true, then the uniqueness, if any, of the biblical God can no longer be found in that combination of universalism and particularism, as was held for so long in certain theological circles.

Rather, it consists in the handling of what I have called the "story of God," and more specifically the part of that story that preceded the post-exilic synthesis of nascent Judaism. Although heavily reworked in the process of synthesis, the books of Amos, Hosea, Micah, Isaiah, Jeremiah, and Ezekiel, and to a lesser extent the books of Kings, are our only sources for pertinent pre-exilic material that might shed some light on our investigation. And an examination of these sources reveals that the difference perceived by them between Yahweh and the other deities did not lie simply in the fact of his deity. Indeed, sometimes they use El terminology and sometimes Baal terminology to refer to him, which was to be expected since Yahweh was either a late or secondary deity in a Canaanite pantheon where El and Baal played the two major roles.

These prophets also reflect, each in his own way, a tendency to perceive Yahweh in terms that actually make him out to be at worst a non-deity and at best a self-destructive deity, when seen against the standards of ancient Near Eastern thought. They claimed that he was independent from his sanctuary and city, i.e., from the seat that made a deity to be a deity. This tendency is already apparent in the teachings of Amos and Hosea. Both, and especially the Judahite Amos, had a golden opportunity to include in their harangues against Bethel the criticism that it represented a schismatic sanctuary, but such a stand is nowhere to be found in either book. In fact, an unwillingness to represent Jerusalem as Yahweh's sole sanctuary must have been a particularly striking and well-established feature of the teachings of those prophets. Consider Amos' editors, who summarized his teaching as the Lord's roaring from *Zion* and uttering his voice from *Jerusalem* against *Carmel* (Am 1:2), and who viewed the ultimate restoration as the raising up of the booth of David (Am 9:11)[11]—even they did not

---

11. The point I am making is even stronger if one concedes that Am 9:11-15 were uttered by Amos himself rather than added by the book's editor.

(dare to?) introduce a pro-Jerusalem stance in the text of Amos' prophecies. This tendency to see Yahweh as independent from his own seat of residence is carried on in Isaiah's teaching (Is 8:6-8) and reaches its peak in Jeremiah's oracles (Jer 7:4). It is just such an idea that must have paved the way for Ezekiel's God whose see is a mobile abode covering the entire breadth of his domain (Ezek 1:11, 14, 19-21, 24).

This independence of Yahweh from his earthly throne could not have been possible unless another kind of abode was secured for him. An overview of the teachings of the same prophets will reveal the nature of this new abode: they all tend to emphasize Yahweh's complete presence in the prophetic word. This was not an entirely new idea. The ancient Near East viewed a seer's *dabar* (word) as having a function similar to a priest's *torah* (instruction) in that each made the deity's will available to the inquirer. However, whereas the *torah* was necessarily linked to a sanctuary through the person of the priest, the seer's *dabar* had the potential of being as itinerant as its bearer. In other words, one and the same deity had two traditionally valid channels of communication, the one more fixed and the other more flexible, at least formally. The novelty in the teaching of Amos and his successors lay in their tendency to give a higher level of authority to their own *dabar* over against the contemporary *torah*, although the content of their *dabar* was highly unorthodox, even heretical. In other words, their *dabar* was intended to challenge and even dislodge the orthodox *torah*. Beginning already with Amos, this was effected through the device of formulating a *dabar* that ironically mimicked a well known *torah* utterance, the point being that the form was similar while the content was utterly contradictory (Am 4:4-5; Is 1:10-15).

Thus, because the teaching of Amos and his successors entailed the demise of the priestly *torah* as the official channel of Yahweh in the eighth, seventh, and sixth centuries B.C., and its substitution with the prophetic *dabar*, it is the person of the prophet himself that took the place of the sanctuary as the official abode of Yahweh. This change manifested itself in two important ways. First the *debarim* (words) of a prophet, while still being presented as the actual *debarim* of Yahweh, as in Amos (Am 1:1; 3:1-2; 4:1-3; 5:1-2), became the hypostasized divine *dabar*, a quasi-independent entity coming to (abide in) the prophet (Hos 1:1;[12] Mic 1:1; Is 2:1; Ezek 1:3). The full swing in thinking is evidenced in the title to the book of Jeremiah which introduces the words of Jeremiah to whom the word of the Lord came (vv.2-3). The other way the change in attitude can be seen is through the editorial passages that speak of the call of Amos and his successors. These show how through the prophets Yahweh himself is quite mobile. Amos is not a prophet, and is a Judahite at that, yet he is made to bear Yahweh's message to Israel (Am 7:1-8:3). Hosea carries the divine message in his flesh, as it were (Hos 1:2-6, 8-9; 2:2-13). The Lord who decides to move out of his sanctuary does so through the medium of Isaiah, and more specifically Isaiah's mouth (Is 6). The same Lord who decides to strike down Jerusalem, the city that contains his sanctuary, can afford to do so since he has conceived Jeremiah himself to be the Lord's own city and the sanctuary of the Lord's own utterances (Jer 1:5, 9, 18-19). Ezekiel provides yet another good example of how the person of the prophet became Yahweh's abode (Ezek 3:1-3, 10): Jerusalem may fall together with its sanctuary, but Yahweh will continue to speak out of his sanctuary by the river Chebar, that is, out of Ezekiel himself (1:1,3). This new sanctuary is handier than the old localized one; it is as ubiquitous as the divine chariot (3:12-15).

Still, the divergence between the priestly *torah* (instruction) and the prophetic *dabar* (word) produced a merger on a different level between these two traditional modes of Yahweh's presence among his people and channels for communicating his will. Al-

12. Compare with 1:2.

though the Deuteronomic reform had its roots in the prophetic teachings, being religious in nature it was naturally championed by the religious leaders in Jerusalem. In fact, some of the prophets were part of that religious leadership (let us remember that Isaiah's call is located in the temple, and that Jeremiah and Ezekiel were priests). Also, the prophetic traditions themselves were preserved and edited into books within the post-exilic priestly circles, the same circles that produced the Pentateuchal *torah* mentioned earlier. That post-exilic *torah* came to have the same characteristics as the prophetic *dabar* in that it was considered essentially independent from any earthly sanctuary. Indeed, its origins were portrayed as being within the wilderness period, around a heavenly sanctuary, and in the midst of an idealized priesthood (Ex 25-40), i.e., even before the historical realities of the kingdoms of Israel and Judah came into existence. Such a portrayal followed the pattern initiated by the Deuteronomists who viewed Moses as a prophet (Deut 18:15, 18) and cast his "prophetic words" into the mold of a definitive *torah* formulated *before* the entry into Canaan. It is clear then that the Pentateuchal *torah*, including the book of Deuteronomy, was conceived as the standard or norm set forth by a thoroughly "independent" deity for yet-to-be kingdoms with their yet-to-be cities and sanctuaries. It is around these two elements of Pentateuchal *torah* and prophetic literature, both the products of post-exilic nascent Judaism, that the notion of *graphe/graphai* evolved.

God's Universalism

By bringing Yahweh's independence from his earthly abode to its logical ultimate conclusion, the exilic and post-exilic Judahites inevitably introduced universalism into the domain of Yahweh's rule. Indeed, beginning with Jeremiah and Ezekiel and culminating with the exilic prophet Second Isaiah, Yahweh's rule was perceived as extending over the Judahites exiled in Babylon and

Egypt as well as over those who remained in Judah. Such an idea meant the expansion of the boundaries of Yahweh's *'eres* to a literally "universal" dimension. This de facto universalism can already be found in the teachings of these three prophets:

1) If Yahweh is capable of ruling over the Judahites outside of Judah, then the Israelites outside Israel are also within his reach. This is why Jeremiah and Ezekiel started speaking of two peoples as two brides of Yahweh. Suddenly, the already long-forgotten Israelite exiles came to be included alongside the Judahite exiles in Yahweh's ultimate plan of salvation from exile and return to Canaan (Jer 3:18; 23:5-6; Ezek 37:15-28).

2) To accomplish this, Yahweh's effective rule had to extend over the Babylonians, and consequently also over other nations. Hence the understanding that Jeremiah was "established as a prophet to the nations" (Jer 1:5) and "established over nations and kingdoms" (v. 10). Hence also the extensive sections of oracles against different nations both in Jeremiah (46-51) and Ezekiel (25-32).[13]

3) Later, according to Second Isaiah, Yahweh even becomes the God of the Medo-Persian Cyrus (Is 44:28-45:7), through whom (Is 46:11) we see that God, rather than Bel/Marduk or Nebo, controls the destiny of Babylon (Is 46:1; Jer 50:2; 51:44). Accordingly, Yahweh's chosen one, the ideal *'ebed* who will perfectly implement this new reality, is his messenger *both* to Israel and to the nations (Is 49:6).

With this de facto universalism, the terms *yahweh* and *'elohim* (God), became co-extensive. Actually, in the final edition of the Pentateuch, *'elohim* became the primary term to refer to the deity honored in pre-exilic Israel and Judah. This is most obvious in the creation account, which is essentially "universal" in nature. Not

---

13. The same was done in the final edition of the book of Isaiah that included teachings of exilic and post-exilic members of his influential "school," thus making the work of that early 7th century B.C. prophet encompass the later crucial period of history beginning with the 6th century.

only is the creator simply *'elohim* in the priestly version (Gen 1:1-2:4a), but also the Yahwistic version (Gen 2:4b-3:24) was systematically revised when it came to the mention of *yahweh*. The more general title *'elohim* was added to all occurrences of the latter personal name so that the creator in this account of creation is not simply the expected *yahweh*, but *yahweh 'elohim*. Interestingly, this priestly retouching of the Pentateuchal Yahwistic tradition is strictly confined to Gen 2-3! On the other hand, it is the name *yahweh* which starts to be added to *'elohim* of the priestly tradition—but only after the "universal" *'elohim* decided to reveal the particular name *yahweh* by which he wanted to be known in Israel and Judah (Ex 6:2-9). Moreover, in the ensuing exodus which is the event of Yahweh's epiphany, Yahweh does not behave as he historically did in Canaan, i.e., battling against other gods. His opponent is Pharaoh rather than the gods of Egypt, the reason being the total lack of other gods in the perspective of the Pentateuchal editor. Thus, in the theological perspective of the Pentateuchal *torah*, the first and most prominent "scripture" of nascent Judaism, the historical process during which the particular *yahweh* became the universal *'elohim* is reversed: one starts with the universal and then introduces the particular.

A striking corollary to the process I have just pointed out is the deliberate toning down and even avoidance of the historical name of the local Canaanite deity. Yahweh became a mere tetragrammaton (a word made of four consonants: *yhwh*) that was read as *'adonay* which simply means "my lord/master." In other words, the name of the deity Yahweh was de-individualized in order to free it to contain the new notion of the universal God. Nascent Judaism took this so seriously that the Septuagint actually translated *'adonay* whenever the Hebrew had *yhwh*, rendering it with the Greek (*ho*) *kyrios* which is a general term referring to a deity in the Hellenistic era. We see the same process in English Bibles, which typically render "the Lord" for Hebrew *yahweh*.

The increasing emphasis on the universality of the biblical God over against his particularism definitely had to do with the rise of "universal" empires, first the Medo-Persian and later the Macedonian. Through the conception and spread of Hellenism, the Macedonian empire paved the way for the one world, the *oikoumene* ([the] inhabited [earth]), of the Roman Empire. The mixture of cultures precipitated by the new empires could have nudged nascent Judaism into practical polytheism, but it didn't. One reason why it didn't had to do with yet another important aspect of ancient Near Eastern kingship: the view of the king as not only the *mošel* (ruler) but also the *šophet* (judge). Of the two, the latter function was ultimately more central to the king's role, because it was connected with the notion of wisdom, i.e., the personal quality that secured the smooth operation and overall well being of the whole kingly realm.[14] It was the more beneficent aspect of kingship, the aspect that ultimately encompassed everybody and everything and brought them together in a harmonious unity. Wisdom was even the element that unified differing kingdoms since it was essentially one and the same, while religions and rules tended to create schisms insofar as deities and rulers are different in different cities. Wisdom's locale was the gates of a city (Pr 1:21; 8:3)[15] which was the place of encounter between people of different classes, traditions, and even kingdoms. It is no wonder then that wisdom became prominent in the thought and concerns of a nascent Judaism which was intent on propagating its idea of one universal God in a world it came to perceive as one. Wisdom was naturally a most convincing channel for that view. Indeed, the Pentateuchal *torah* itself came to be presented as divine wisdom.[16] It was only a matter of time before wisdom literature became the third element within the *graphe/graphai* of Judaism.

14. The three essential functions of the king as ruler, priest, and dispenser of wisdom are clearly underlined in the paradigmatic depiction of Solomon, the king par excellence (1 Kg 3-10). The prominence of wisdom is indicated by the fact that it is mentioned first.
15. See ch.9.
16. Sir 11:15; 15:1; 19:20; 21:11; 24:23f; 2 Esd 8:12; 13:54f.; 4 Macc 1:15ff. See chs.10 and 12.

The New Testament

The New Testament clearly reflects a belief that through Jesus of Nazareth, the *oikonomia* (plan, intent) of the one God of the Old Testament has reached its final stage.[17] Even a cursory reading of this early Christian literature would suffice to convince one of the truth of that assertion. The obvious assumption is that these two sets of writings constitute one *graphe*. The question to be considered is then: Is there an inner correspondence between the texture of the New Testament and that of the Old Testament so as to make such an assumption tenable? I believe there is.

First, as was the case with the Old Testament, what holds the New Testament together as a unity is what was originally an extra-biblical premise, in this case the oneness and universality of the lordship of Jesus. A closer look at the New Testament writings will show that this premise was developed through a similar process as the one that had been followed in the Old Testament. Just as the local, "historical," individual deity Yahweh came to be viewed as the universal God, in the same way it was the historical, individual man Jesus that came to be viewed as the universal Lord. As evidence for this, consider the fact that (a) the gospels, whose subject matter is the pre-Easter Jesus, amount to nearly half of the New Testament, and (b) the rest of the New Testament literature assumes the actual teaching of that pre-Easter Jesus even when it does not refer to it directly. Tacitly or implicitly, all of these texts give primary importance to the meaning of Jesus' crucifixion and death. Put otherwise, just as the universal God was understood on the basis of the Canaanite deity Yahweh, the universal Lord was understood on the basis of Jesus of Nazareth. Or if one prefers the more traditional terminology of revelation: divine revelation is at

17. The debate as to whether this is true or not is immaterial to my argument. Actually, the truth of that matter is and will always remain as debatable as the truth of the Old Testament premise regarding the existence of the biblical God, let alone his oneness and universality.

work according to the very same mechanism in both the Old
Testament and the New Testament.

On the other hand, however, the premise of the lordship of
Jesus assumes the premise—scriptural by now—of the oneness
and universality of God. (Actually, these two characteristics necessarily go together; they *always* function together, as if they were
two foci of an ellipse.) But what is important for our discussion is
the way in which the New Testament premise is handled by the
biblical authors. They present Jesus to us in terms of one or
another of the ways in which God himself is identified in the Old
Testament books. Specifically, the New Testament writers refer to
Jesus in terms of the Pentateuchal *torah*, the prophetic *dabar*, and
wisdom. When I say "in terms of," I do not mean simply that they
use such terms, but that they actually present him as being *himself*
(a) either the new *torah* or its dispenser as only God would be;[18]
(b) either the divine *dabar* or its source as only God would be;[19]
and (c) divine wisdom.[20] Consequently, the intended message is
unmistakable: Jesus is presented to the reader in the New Testament in the same way in which God is in the Old Testament.

It was necessary that the belief in Jesus' lordship be based upon
Yahweh's lordship, since Jesus was a human being while Yahweh
was a deity. But what is more important is that as a human being
Jesus functioned also as the medium through whom God implemented his revelation. Accordingly, Jesus is depicted in the New
Testament as another Moses,[21] a high priest,[22] a prophet,[23] a
Messiah, i.e., as being each and every one of the classical channels
for God in the Judaic *graphe*. The last two are especially prominent because they were the ways Jesus' contemporaries viewed

18. See, e.g., Mt 5:20-48; Mt 12:8//Mk 2:28//Lk 6:5.
19. See, e.g., Jn 1:1; 1 Jn 1:1.
20. See, e.g., 1 Cor 1:30; 2:7-8; also Lk 7:31-35.
21. See, e.g., Mt 19:1-9.
22. See, e.g., Heb 2:17; 3:1; 4:14-15.
23. See, e.g., Mt 21:10-11; Lk 7:16; Jn 6:14; 7:40.

him during the years of his ministry. And no wonder, since the eschatological prophet (as the rekindler of the long-quenched spirit of God) and the Messiah were in first century A.D. Judaism the two classical figures linked to the advent and establishment of God's kingdom. And that kingdom was none other than the realization of God's *oikonomia* as it was witnessed to in the Judaic *graphe*. The conclusion is inescapable: the Old Testament God not only continues his revelation and *oikonomia* in Jesus, but also "ends" them in the sense that their ultimate goal has been realized in Jesus.

A digression is in order here. Recent biblical scholarship has revealed the centrality for New Testament thought of the notion of wisdom, more specifically of Jesus as hypostasized divine wisdom. This identification was handy for the New Testament authors on two planes. On the one hand, it helped promote a conception of Jesus as divine. The notion of *kyrios* (lord) by itself risked either making him just one more *kyrios* among many (see 1 Cor 8:4-6; Eph 1:21; Col 1:16; 2:15) or fully identifying him with the Old Testament *kyrios,* i.e., God himself. Wisdom provided a safeguard against either pitfall: it reflected the fact that Jesus partook of the divinity of the one true God as opposed to that of the "other gods," yet did not confuse him with God the Father. On the other hand, as I indicated earlier, wisdom had an *oikonomical* function in the Old Testament. It paved the way for the idea of God's universality by including within the realm of his sovereignty the other nations, which inclusion was viewed as an integral feature of the eschatological realization of God's kingdom (Is 2:1-5; 49:6; 66:18; 61:11; Mic 4:1-3; Zech 14). In a similar way, the acceptance of the Gentiles under God's aegis was a central theme for the early church's gospel, notwithstanding the different approaches taken by Paul and the Jerusalem Jewish-Christian authorities (Gal 2). And in the same way, wisdom theology played a role in this, along with the related notion of the divine mystery hidden before the ages and revealed at the end of time through the apostles (Rom 16:25; 1 Cor 4:1; Eph 1:9; 3:3-4, 9; 6:19; Col 1:26f.; 2:2-3; 4:3; Rev 10:7).

One cannot help but conclude that the parameters of the early church's view of Jesus were the same as those within which the idea of hypostasized divine wisdom arose in nascent Judaism. But, as I indicated earlier, this idea goes hand in hand with the core of nascent Judaism, namely the belief in the one and universal God. In other words, what the early church believed happened in Jesus, it saw as the goal and therefore the *terminus ad quem* of the "movement" initiated by nascent Judaism.

Taken together, all of the preceding conclusions make it crystal clear that in the New Testament writings we find not only a continuation of the "story" of the Old Testament God, but a continuation that brings this "story" to its end. The Judaic God is, as it were, exhaustively presented—or more traditionally speaking, exhaustively presents himself—in Jesus. Consequently, (a) the New Testament may not be conceived as independent scripture, and (b) if scripture at all, then it must also be taken as the concluding part of the Judaic scripture.

The Unity of the Bible

The fact that Old Testament and New Testament form one scripture in their common texture is corroborated by the uniqueness of the phenomenon of the New Testament within Judaism. Indeed, the literary products of all other branches of Judaism extant until 70 A.D. amounted to nothing at all like the New Testament. They consisted of (a) debates around, comments on, and footnotes to various parts of what was considered to be scripture at the time (e.g., the rabbinic tradition); or (b) commentaries on some of its books (e.g., Qumran, Philo); or (c) reviews of those books, intending to present "histories of the Jews" (e.g., Josephus); or (d) rules concerning the inner life of a particular community (e.g., Qumran). Of all this literature none came to be considered scripture. Not even the Talmudic literature of post-70 A.D. came to be considered as scripture. We will never know what the shape, content, and limits of the non-Christian Judaic scripture would have been had the catastrophe of 70 A.D. not taken place. But it is safe to say that the destruction of Jerusalem and its temple would not have been, by itself, reason enough to cause post-70 A.D. rabbinic Judaism to close its scriptural canon the way it did. We need only remember the fact that the previous catastrophe of 587 B.C. actually triggered the production of canonical scriptures. So why did rabbinic Judaism close the canon?

It was no doubt a reaction to the rise within Judaism of a movement that produced new scriptures which brought the "story" of the scriptural God, and thus of Judaism's scripture itself, to an end. After A.D. 70 this new movement could not be contained and so could not be ignored. Why might rabbinic Judaism have felt that the new Judaic movement should have been contained? Because, by bringing to an end the "story" of God and of scripture, it actually brought the "history" of Judaism, which is inherently connected with scripture and its God, to an end. The destruction of Jerusalem provided evidence that tended to support that thesis, thereby giving Judaism more incentive to oppose the new movement.

Now, while the Christians saw in Jesus the end of the "story of God," they understood "end" in the sense of "goal" or "purpose" rather than simply "termination." Indeed, the end of any "story" or "history" cannot be equivalent to its demise, as if its subject matter never existed. Rather the "story" or "history" of a particular reality reaches its end when the ultimate meaning of that reality is revealed, i.e., when there is nothing more that can shed light on the subject of what this reality is *all about*. It is in this sense that God, the scriptural canon, and even post-exilic nascent Judaism itself find their end in Jesus, according to the perspective of the New Testament texts. It is, of course, impossible to prove or disprove the truth or validity of this point of view; it can only be witnessed to. And that is what the scriptural texts do: they witness to the truth.

The duty of one whose mind has been baptized into the perspective of the one Bible is to witness to the same truth and adopt the same perspective. To do so he must delve into its reality; he must learn it so thoroughly that it becomes entirely his own reality. And this biblical reality prohibits him, *when dealing with the Bible and its truth*, from speaking in the non-biblical terminology according to which Christianity and contemporary Judaism are religions. As such, these categories are totally alien to the biblical mindset. Those of us who have been baptized into the biblical Jesus Christ must witness to the one biblical God of the one scripture at whatever cost. And this God is entirely contained in this scripture, since his *entire* "history" is contained in it. Any extension of him and his revelatory activity beyond the confines of the one scripture will make out of him the product of our own premise regarding godhead, and will thus bind him to the fetters of our creative imagination. Conversely, any dissection of the one scripture into independent parts will produce the same result. And the baptized Christian who is tempted to make concessions to modern theological trends must always remember that he is the servant of the biblical Jesus Christ and of the latter's God and Father, not their public relations manager.

15

The Authority of the Old Testament

The Old and New Testaments constitute one book, but they are nevertheless distinct parts of that book. Should a Christian view them also as having distinctly different levels of scriptural authority? Since this question was raised by Marcion, the second-century A.D. heretic, debate on the topic has never died. A wide range of answers have been proposed, ranging from considering the Old Testament as ultimately the only real scripture to viewing it as totally irrelevant.

To begin with, one may not disregard the early, common, patristic tradition that spoke of the *entire* scripture, both Old and New Testaments, as the *one* "Word of God." In other words, as in any other religion, the *one* Christian faith is bound by its one Bible. Thus, the Old Testament books are as much "biblical" as those of the New Testament. The former were read in the gatherings, preached on, taught, commented upon, used in the creeds, etc., in the same vein as the latter were. In the third century, Origen, an official teacher at the official school of the Alexandrian church (the second most important church after the Roman one) spent much energy trying to figure out what the original text of the Old Testament was. He put side by side[1] all the available material in Hebrew as well as in Greek, and compared them. Why would he do that if he, and the church of Alexandria with him, did not consider the Old Testament text to be the "Word of God"?

Yet how can one put on the same level of authority the New Testament which witnesses directly to Jesus the Christ our Lord, and the Old Testament which only looks forward to him?[2] The

---

1. In six columns in His Hexapla and in eight in His Octapla.

2. One need only recall, for instance, the case of circumcision and cultic rules that have been abrogated by the New Testament, to perceive the importance of this matter.

solution lies in the realization that the Christian is never faced directly with the person of Christ, but rather with the *text* of the New Testament. For him, both *texts*, Old Testament and New Testament, speak of Christ. The former text delineates the features of the scriptural God's Christ and the latter text witnesses to the fact that it is Jesus of Nazareth, son of Mary, who is the Christ because *those features apply to him*. Thus, for a Christian the contents of these two can only be understood together, not separately.

Let me take the very difficult example of circumcision to prove my point. Abrahamic circumcision in Genesis 17 is *in the flesh*, but not fleshly, i.e., human; otherwise, how could one explain that any circumcised person becomes Abraham's child and a member of God's community through a mere "fleshly" operation? In other words, the "Word of God" for us lies in the *meaning* given circumcision in the Old Testament, and not in circumcision itself which was, after all, common among many ancient Near Eastern peoples.[3] And its basic meaning is that God's fatherhood was granted *freely* to anyone who would accept it (Gen 17:12-14). This is precisely what Paul argued for in Galatians 3-4 and this is precisely the meaning given baptism and the gift of the Spirit in the New Testament.[4] In other words, Genesis 17 is not tangentially, but essentially, still valid for us today: it is there that we, as children of Abraham, hear of God's free gift to us. Baptism better be biblical circumcision for us, else it will not be baptism at all!

But, one might object, even as texts the Old and New Testaments are not fully similar: the former still looks forward, while the latter looks backward, to Christ. Actually, both of them look forward in the same way. In which sense does the Old Testament look forward? The answer unequivocally is: first and foremost it does so *essentially*. Every text that is considered authoritative is addressed to the community that considers it so. But, in which

3. See, e.g., Jer 9:25-26.
4. See e.g. Rom 4:11; 8:14-16; Eph 4:30.

sense would a text speaking of bygone events be of interest to a present community, unless it is of essence for the *future* of this community? This is exactly, to take just one example, how the Declaration of Independence, the Constitution of the United States of America, and its Bill of Rights operate for a citizen of the USA. The Declaration of Independence is important now not only as a historical record but as an expression of ideals the U.S. holds and plans to continue to live by both now and in the future. That is, *functionally* an authoritative text always "looks forward," "toward the future" of the intended community. This is precisely what we have discovered in our study of the different Old Testament traditions, and the same obviously applies to the New Testament. Not only the epistles, but also the gospels, although about Jesus, were definitely written for the edification—and thus the future life—of their contemporary communities:

> Inasmuch as many have undertaken to compile a narrative of the things which have been accomplished among us, just as they were delivered to us by those who from the beginning were eyewitnesses and ministers of the word, it seemed good to me also, having followed all things closely for some time past, to write an orderly account for you, most excellent Theophilus, that you may know the truth concerning the things of which you have been informed. (Lk 1:1-4)

> Now Jesus did many other signs in the presence of the disciples, which are not written in this book; but these are written that you may believe that Jesus is the Christ, the Son of God, and that believing you may have life in his name. (Jn 20:30-31)

However, there is a difference between the authoritative documents of the USA and the Old Testament in that for the latter the future is not open-ended. Rather, it is determined by the Lord of scriptures himself, who will come to save as well as to judge primarily those to whom these scriptures are addressed. This feature is so essential to these scriptures that even the event of his coming in Jesus of Nazareth produced a second set of scriptures, the New Testament, made out of the same fabric: the believers are faced with the coming Christ and Lord Jesus. So, in both cases of the Old and New Testaments, the events referred to are behind us, but the future judgment and salvation that faced our "fathers," i.e. predecessors, and witnessed to in these scriptures, are about to face *us* this time around.

In the case of nascent Judaism, its adherents were addressed by the Old Testament that told them of the events in which God faced their fathers. They had no personal experience of those events and so could only "experience" them through the "word" of scripture.[5] In our case, the New Testament tells *us* of the way God faced *them* with his "Word," the scriptures of the Old Testament. That is why in our case God's "Word" of judgment as well as of salvation is final and thus irreversible: God's New Testament "Word" witnesses to the fulfillment of his Old Testament "Word" of judgment and salvation. In the New Testament scriptures we continually stand before God's Word "fulfilled", i.e., with no possibility of anything beyond it and consequently no chance for appeal of any sort for whoever has accepted it. In this case, misunderstanding God's Word can only be a lame excuse. By confessing that something is fulfilled we do not "magically" come to understand it through a "magical" inner light that suddenly shines in a "magical" manner into our "magical" mind. This would put us above God's Word! It is rather by studying the Word, by working hard to understand it without attaching to it any of our preconceived notions about it, that we have the chance to perceive correctly the way in which it attained its fulfillment.[6] The Old Testament is to be read—actually heard and hearkened to—as the *authoritative* Word of God that *authoritatively shapes our minds* in order to enable us to comprehend its coming to full fruition in the *equally authoritative* New Testament Word of God. Only by doing so and thus training ourselves to view our God, the biblical God, always in terms of his coming to save and judge, as

5. See vol.2, pp.213-214.
6. See the Epilogues to vol.1 and vol.2.

the Old Testament teaches us time and again, will we stand the chance of realizing that he has graciously already done so "once and for all" in Jesus of Nazareth and that it would already be too late for us, were it not for his fatherly mercy toward the just and the unjust, since neither will ever be as perfect as he is.[7]

7. See Mt 5:43-48.

Selected Bibliography

M. Dahood, *Psalms I, Psalms II* and *Psalms III*, Garden City, 1965, 1968 and 1970.

J. H. Eaton, *Kingship and the Psalms*, London.

E. S. Gesterberger, *Psalms* (fotl) Grand Rapids, 1988.

H.-J. Kraus, *Psalms 1-59* and *Psalms 60-150*, Minneapolis, 1988 and 1989.

C. Westermann, *The Psalms: Structure, Content, and Message*, Minneapolis, 1981.

J. L. Crenshaw, *Old Testament Wisdom*, Atlanta, 1981

R. E. Murphy, *Wisdom Literature: Job ,Proverbs, Ruth, Canticles, Ecclesiastes, Esther* (fotl), Grand Rapids, 1981.

G. von Rad, *Wisdom in Israel*, Nashville, 1972.

R. B. Y. Scott, *The Way of Wisdom*, New York, 1971.

R. Gordis, *The Book of Job*, New York, 1978.

N. C. Habel, *The Book of Job*, Philadelphia, 1985.

C. Westermann, *The Structure of the Book of Job*, Philadelphia, 1981.

R. N. Whybray, *Two Jewish Theologies: Job and Ecclesiastes*, Hull, 1980.

William McKane, *Proverbs* (OTL), Philadelphia, 1970.

B. Lang, *Wisdom and the Book of Proverbs*, New York, 1986.

R. N. Whybray, *Wisdom in Proverbs*, London, 1972.

J. L. Crenshaw, *Ecclesiastes* (OTL), Phildelphia, 1987.

R. Gordis, *Kohelet: The Man and His World*, New York, 1968.

G. S. Ogden, *Qohelet*, Sheffield, 1987.

J. M. Reese, *The Book of Wisdom, Song of Songs* (OTM), Wilmington, 1983.

R. A. F. McKenzie, *Sirach* (OTM), Wilmington, 1983.

Index of Scriptural References

Index of Subjects